GHOSTS AND HAUNTS

*** *of the* ***

CIVIL WAR

GHOSTS AND HAUNTS

HAUNTS

*** *of the* ***

CIVIL WAR

AUTHENTIC ACCOUNTS OF THE STRANGE AND UNEXPLAINED

CHRISTOPHER K. COLEMAN

BARNES
&NOBLE
BOOKS
NEW YORK

To my beautiful wife Veronica:
Thanks for all your love, patience, and help.

CONTENTS

ACKNOWLEDGMENTS

I would like to express my appreciation to the staff of the Metropolitan Nashville Public Library and especially the Area Resource Center and Local History Room staff for all their help in researching this book. Likewise, the Tennessee State Library and Archives has also been most helpful.

A number of individuals were of valuable service in my quest to document Civil War ghosts and haunts: among them Mr. Paul Chiles of Sharpsburg, Maryland; for information on Antietam; Patty O'Day at Farnsworth House, Gettysburg; Shirley Dougherty, of Harper's Ferry, West Virginia; Louise Mudd Arehart of Maryland; Ruth Fitzgerald of Smith-Trahern House, Clarksville, Tennessee; Susan McDowell of Belle Grove Mansion, Virginia; Blanche Terry of the Old Court House, Vicksburg, Mississippi and Mr. Walt Grayson, Mississippi film producer.

INTRODUCTION

An event as significant as the Civil War cannot fail to leave its mark on America. More than just another era in history, it has affected all aspects of our society, culture, and consciousness.

While it is easy enough to point to a host of material consequences of the War Between the States, it is not so easy to find the very real mark it has left upon the invisible realm of the spirit. The fact that this impact is less apparent does not make it any less real, however. Untold physical anguish and suffering, premature and violent death, emotional turmoil are all fertile ground for the creation of psychic phenomena of one sort or another. Certainly no single event, save perhaps the American Revolution, has had such a profound impact on the United States.

Throughout the South, there is hardly a community that cannot claim at least one ghost or other psychic phenomena somehow related to the Civil War. But the supernatural impact of the war has been documented far beyond the bounds of Dixie—from the Midwest to Boston Harbor. Aspects of the supernatural Civil War include far more than haunted houses or battlefields and extend in time from well before to well after the war itself.

Needless to say, you will not find any of the following incidents described by any mainstream historians. Although many of these events are amply documented in the contemporary record, they have been studiously ignored by academia.

The fact of the matter is, that one does not receive tenure as a professor, or become a department chairman at a major university, by propounding outlandish ideas—no matter how true they may be. One is reminded of Galileo, charged with heresy and forced to deny the earth revolved around the sun, a fact he knew to be true.

Though human existence is short, there is a realm beyond which stretches to infinity, where memories endure; and it is this realm we shall dare to visit. But if life is brief, our journey is long; so let us go then, you and I, while we may, and explore the shadowy side of the Civil War.

GHOSTS AND HAUNTS OF THE CIVIL WAR

*Authentic Accounts of the
Strange and Unexplained*

PART ONE
VISIONS OF THE
COMING STORM

To us, viewing the Civil War with the hindsight of a century and a half or more, the conflict seems like an inevitable thing with all the events preceding it leading logically up to the conflict. But that is not so.

For most folks, the issues of the day were important, even crucial; yet most people could not conceive that the country would actually go to war with itself until it actually happened. There were those, however, for whom the veil of the future was pulled aside, if only for a moment, and they saw the whole thing clearly. Some, possessed of darker visions, tried to force the issue to come sooner, seeking to bend destiny to their own will. Either way, they all were possessed of a vision far beyond mortal ken.

1

GOING TO JERUSALEM: THE REVELATIONS OF NATHAN TURNER

A t his birth, there were portents; all agreed on that much. But whether those signs portended great good or great evil depends on one's point of view. Either way, Nathan's birth and early childhood were accompanied by indications that he was no ordinary person. For one thing, there were certain marks on his head and breast at birth, which his family and neighbors took to be a divine sign.

When Nathan—or Nat—was but three years old, he began to exhibit knowledge of things that had happened long before he was born, and without having had a lesson, or being taught the alphabet, Nat seemed able to read with the most perfect facility.

Nat would certainly have gone far in the world, gifted as he was with great intelligence, an inquiring and inventive mind, and demonstrable leadership abilities, save for one thing: Nat Turner was born a slave. Nat was born on October 2, 1800, the property of one Benjamin Turner of Southampton County, Virginia. Whites and blacks quickly noticed Nat's precociousness—prodigy is more like it—his white master said ominously that Nat "had too much sense to be raised," and the black folks declared that he "surely would be a prophet," since the Lord had shown him things that had happened before he was born. Whenever he got a chance, Nat would sneak a peek at a book (such things were forbidden to slaves), and he would often find, while reading of some new device or invention, that he had already conceived of that very thing on his own, so agile and quick was his mind.

As he grew, all the blacks in the neighborhood came to regard Nat Turner with awe and wonder; looking to him for both guidance and leadership. "Having soon discovered to be great, I must appear so, and therefore studiously avoided mixing in society, and wrapped myself in mystery," Nat confessed. When he was not hard at work in the fields, Nat devoted himself to almost constant prayer and fasting. As he studied the Bible, one passage in particular caught his attention: "Seek ye the Kingdom of Heaven and all things shall be added unto you."

As he was praying at the plough one day, Nat heard a voice—a spirit voice—speaking to him. Nat believed it was of divine origin—the spirit, he fancied, who had spoken to the prophets in former days—and he was greatly astonished. Praying and fasting continually for two more years, Nat heard the same revelations again spoken to him, confirming in his mind and others his role as prophet. Nat would tell his fellow slaves of the various revealed truths that had come to him, and he was held in great awe by them as seer and prophet.

When Nat Turner arrived at a man's estate, he began to turn his attention to the great object, the divine purpose, for which he was sure he had been divinely ordained. Nat was now in almost constant communication with "the Spirit." Whether this spirit was divine or demonic, however, remains a matter of speculation.

In 1825, a new overseer was appointed to the plantation, with whom Nat was soon at odds, and like his father before him, Nat Turner fled, becoming a fugitive slave. It seems clear, granted his intelligence, that Nathan could probably have gotten away clean. But the spirit chided Nat for running away—fleeing was not the fate the spirit had in store for him. To the amazement and consternation of the other slaves, Nat returned to bondage voluntarily, for he realized that was where his destiny now lay.

At about this time, Nat had a great revelation. The sun darkened, the thunder rolled in the heavens, and blood flowed in the rivers. Nat witnessed a vision of white and black spirits engaged in battle, and over it all he heard a voice say, "Such is your luck, such you are called to see, and let it come, rough or smooth, you must surely bear it." Knowledge of the elements was revealed to him, and the revolutions of the planets, the operation of tides, and the changes of season—all the secrets of the natural world became as an open book to Nat. He also developed the gift of healing, both spiritual and physical.

Nat told Ethelred Brantley, a white man, of his revelations and Nat's words had a transforming effect. Brantley had blood ooze from his skin—stigmata—and then was made whole again. Brantley ceased his wickedness.

More revelations followed. In 1828, the spirit again spoke to Nat and informed him, "the Serpent is loosed." Nat now knew the time was fast approaching when the "last shall be first." The time to commence his "work" would be revealed by a sign in the heaven. That sign would not be long in coming. In February of 1828, a full eclipse of the sun occurred. Nat Turner knew at last his time had come.

Among those things promised by the spirit, if Nat Turner was obedient to its will, was that it would lead him and his followers to Jerusalem and they would be justified.

By the beginning of 1830, Nat was living with Joseph Travis's family. By Nat's own admission, Travis had been kind to him, placing the greatest trust in him. Nat had no cause for complaint against him. On the evening of August 21, 1831, however, Nat and several of his followers had a feast in the forest and at that meeting finalized their plans.

That same night, Nat and his followers snuck into the Travis home and, one by one, hacked to death Mr. and Mrs. Travis and all their sleeping children. After they had traveled some distance from the blood-drenched house, they remembered that in their frenzy, they had forgotten about an infant in a cradle who had slept through the slaughter. Will and Henry, two of Nat's trusted followers, went back and hacked the baby up as well.

The insurgents had agreed that "until [they] had armed and equipped [them]selves and gathered suffi-cient force, neither age nor sex was to be spared." Nat and his small rebel slave army were most zealous in carrying out this rule, for the spirit was on their side, and it had promised them that if they followed its com-mands, they would enter Jerusalem and be justified.

As they marched across the countryside, anyone with white skin was cut down. Those who were shot were lucky. Most victims were hacked and slashed to death with dull axes. A boarding school for young girls was assailed, and the girls, all asleep and unarmed at the time, were hacked to death by the insurgents. Scores of other innocent whites also fell beneath their axes and kitchen knives.

As the band progressed in its rampage across the countryside, they obtained horses, ammunition, and a few guns. They soon grew to nineteen; then others joined them, and soon they were able to muster sixty men, all mounted and armed with a variety of deadly weapons.

Wherever they went, Nat Turner and his men brought death and destruction. Soon word spread of the slave revolt, and the rebels encountered a posse of armed men gathered to resist them. A running fight ensued with both sides taking losses.

Nat retreated to collect his scattered army and to seek out new recruits. He still had faith in his mission. Had not the spirit spoken to him? Had it not promised they would be justified? Turner was forced to fall back temporarily—but his goal was still unchanged. On to Jerusalem!

Nat Turner recruited more slaves and rallied his scattered troops till they again amounted to some forty men. By now, all the white farmers were alerted to the menace and had fled the countryside, leaving Nat and his rebel army, masters of all they surveyed—for the moment.

Even as the insurgents camped at Major Ridley's abandoned house, the governor of Virginia had summoned the state militia to deal with the uprising, and local bands of armed whites on their own were also combing the countryside in search of Nat Turner—and vengeance.

Elsewhere in the South, other slave revolts had broken out about the same time, and for awhile it seemed as though there were some great conspiracy afoot. White Southerners' darkest fears had been confirmed, it seemed, by Nat Turner's revolt.

Still intending to pursue his course, Nat led his men onward again. Now, however, they were no longer facing unarmed women and children, or families asleep in their beds, but heavily armed bands of men with one thought on their minds: getting Nat Turner.

His little army, knowing the enemy was rapidly closing in on them on all sides, began to melt away, first at Major Ridley's place and later on encountering resistance at Captain Harris's farm. Soon, Nat was reduced to the handful of rebels he had started with.

It was not long before even these few followers were gone, either killed or fled. For six weeks, Nat Turner still evaded the search parties trying to hunt him down, but in the end he was caught, convicted and condemned to death.

To the end, Nat Turner avowed that the spirit had directed him in all his actions—that it had given him revelations. To the very end, Nat Turner remained convinced of the veracity of what the spirit had told him.

The spirit—whatever it was—regarding at least one particular had spoken true. It had promised Nat that he would be justified and that it would lead him to Jerusalem. Nat Turner was imprisoned, tried, and finally executed . . . in Jerusalem, Virginia.

2

THAR'S A DAY A-COMIN'

It has long been the fashion among both historians and folklorists to make light of the supernatural beliefs and practices that had been traditionally observed in the African-American community. Dismissed as ignorance and superstition, these practices and their practitioners have rarely been taken seriously. Yet well before any armies of blue and gray clashed in bloody battle, there were those in the black community who saw it all coming; they saw it with an inner light as clear and lucid as the morning light of a new day.

From the earliest days of the South, almost every African-American community has had at least one person thought to possess psychic powers. Such persons were both feared and revered, as well they should have been; practitioners of root medicine and fashioners of love charms, on occasion they could also cast a more malicious spell, if so moved. And many, so empowered with the dark arts, also had the gift of prophecy. They were often the benign, seemingly innocuous "Aunt" or "Uncle" so familiar to plantation society.

For the most part, their pronouncements about the future have gone unnoticed by history, as no one cared enough to write them down. But there is at least one recorded instance where such pronouncements, demonstrating a visual clarity of the future, were spoken and cannot be dismissed as mere superstition.

Before the Civil War, it was not uncommon for well-to-do Southern families to secure the services of young, well-educated young ladies from the North to serve as governesses for their children. In 1839, a New England girl of nineteen, named Mary, had secured such a position, tending to the three children of a wealthy planter.

The chief housekeeper of this household was a dignified black woman named Aunt Aggy. Unlike some of the other house servants, she was neither talkative, nor fawning; rather, she maintained a grave but respectful demeanor and was completely trusted. In addition to doing her daily household chores, Aunt Aggy acted as a nurse and foster mother to Miss Lucy, Miss Mary, and "Massa" Robert—the planter's children.

One summer morning, Aunt Aggy's only daughter, Caroline, a pretty and graceful young girl of creamy complexion, was serving breakfast to the master and his family in the dining room. As she was passing a cup of coffee to the master, the planter's hand accidentally knocked the cup from the tray she was holding, spewing coffee all over his linen pants, scalding him badly.

Jumping out of his chair and hurling obscene curses at the young girl, he grabbed a chair and began pounding Caroline with it. Knocking her to the floor with the force of his blows, he continued striking her with the splintered fragments of the chair even after she lay unconscious on the floor.

Poor Caroline was carried, senseless, bruised, and bleeding, to Aunt Aggy's cottage. Mary, the governess, horrified at the savagery she had just witnessed, left the table, withdrawing to her own apartment.

Later that day, Aunt Aggy came to Mary's room on a household errand. Mary took the opportunity to express her indignation to Aggy at the brutal treatment of her daughter.

Aunt Aggy turned squarely about and faced Mary, her large lustrous eyes ablaze with emotion. A dramatic change came over Aunt Aggy, as if some outside entity had taken over her body and was speaking through her.

Raising her right hand to heaven like a biblical prophet, she spoke with a strange otherworldly voice. "Thar's a day a-comin'! Thar's a day a-comin'!" she said. "I hear de rumblin' ob de chariots! I see de flashin' ob de guns! White folks' blood is a-runnin' on de ground like a riber, an' de dead's heaped up dat high!" With her hand she measured at the level of her shoulder the invisible pile of corpses.

"Oh Lord," she said, "hasten de day when de blows, an' de bruises, an' de aches, an' de pains shall come to de white folks, an' de buzzards eat 'em as dey's dead in de streets. Oh, Lord! Roll on de chariots, an' git de black people rest an' peace."

It would be more than a score of years before Aunt Aggy's prophecy would come to fruition; but come true it did; the chariots did indeed roll on. Mary left the employ of the rich planter and returned north, now a confirmed abolitionist. She married, becoming Mrs. Livermore, and settled in Chicago.

The outbreak of the war found Mary Livermore active with the Sanitary Commission, doing her utmost to help suffering Union soldiers and their families, and various victims of the war.

As fate would have it, she and Aunt Aggy crossed paths once more. Late in the war, Mary was visiting a "contraband" camp near Washington, D.C., where blacks who had fled slavery were living and working. One day, at a religious meeting in camp, she encountered the elderly Aggy. At the close of the prayer meeting, Mary could not help but mention the beating of Caroline witnessed long before. Mary learned from Aggy that time—or the Lord—had not been kind to the cruel master and his family.

"Ol' massa and missus bof done died," she told Mrs. Livermore, "an' young Massa Robert . . . he done died in des yer arms. Little Massa Batt . . . he went to de war an' was shot in ole Carolina, an' buerd wid his sojers." And so it was with all the other members of the family— dead of one cause or another, the plantation all broken up, and the slave population spread to the four winds.

Aunt Aggy was correct about the shades of war she had visioned long before. "I allers knowed it was a-comin', I allers heerd de rumblin' o' de wheels. I allers 'spected to see white folks heaped up dead. An' de Lord He's kept his promise, an' avenged His people, jus' as I knowed He would," she told Mary.

The incident from 1839 had seared the memory of both women, and both well remembered the prophetic words uttered that day. For Aggy and Mary there was little doubt that the veil which separated present and future had been lifted, enabling the old Black woman to become like the seers of old.

As Aggy declared to Mary before they parted ways again, "Oh, de Lord, He do jes' right, if you only gib Him time enough to turn Hisself."

3

THE FATAL VISION OF MAMMY WISE

In the South, premonitions and visions of the onset of the Civil War were not unique to one race. In the mountains of Appalachia, there is a long tradition of individuals believed to possess the "gift"—folk able to cure the sick, spell up solutions to people's personal problems, and sometimes even predict the future.

Back in the 1930s, the federal government hired a number of young folk to collect oral history and local folklore all across the South. At that time, there were still a good many people who could vividly remember the war—including all the things the historians left out.

One young worker, gathering material for the Works Progress Administration (W.P.A.) Writers' Project in Tennessee, came across an old "wise woman" who gave a unique explanation of how the War Between the States came about.

They called her Mammy Wise, and while that was not her Christian name, it fit her well. She lived in the Great Valley of east Tennessee, and by all accounts, was as old as the hills and mountains that surrounded it.

Untold generations came and went, and for as long as anyone could remember Mammy Wise could be seen a-rockin' away on her porch, smoking her old corn-cob pipe. Her great size and thick snowy-white hair were in stark contrast to her small black eyes and her leathery skin—tanned as dark as an Indant's by scores of years working in the fields.

It was with some apprehension that Julia Wilhout, a young W.P.A. worker, approached the weathered old cabin where Mammy Wise held court. Julia was not sure if anyone was at home. People in that part of the country were still wary of strangers and downright hostile to government folk. Julia needn't have worried, though. Mammy Wise was used to people knocking on her door at all hours of the day and night. New mothers came to her to cure their baby of the thrush; others would seek her out to sooth up lost or stolen objects; even spinsters well past their teens knew that if anyone could spell up a husband for them, Mammy Wise could.

Julia gathered abundant material from the venerable "wise woman" that day. Many weird and wondrous things were credited to Mammy Wise and her trances. But knowledge can be a dangerous thing—all the more so when people fail to heed your warnings.

One day, well before the war, Mammy Wise went into a fit. It was a trance greater and more intense than any she'd had before. In her vision, she saw a star from the northern sky soar across the heavens and collide with a star in the south end of the sky.

To any who would listen, she would warn them: "trouble is a-brewin' betwixt the north end of America and the south end of America." Folks in the Valley knew that whatever Mammy Wise spelled up always came true, but none of the politicians took her warnings seriously.

The war did come, of course, just the way Mammy Wise had predicted it. Mammy Wise always felt bad about spellin' that one up. After that, she said she was always "right careful about what she dreamed on."

4

THE BLACK SPOT

If any man can lay claim to being the godfather of secessionism, surely it's John C. Calhoun of South Carolina. Throughout his career in Congress, Calhoun was a fierce proponent of states' rights. It was Calhoun who proposed the doctrine that individual states were autonomous domains whose laws took precedence over those of the federal government.

Oddly though, toward the end of his career, this inflexible defender of sectionalism and state sovereignty made an abrupt about-face. From his unyielding opposition to federal authority, Calhoun suddenly became an advocate for a new nationalism where sectional differences would be subordinated to the good of the nation as a whole.

Calhoun's former supporters spurned his new ideas, however, repudiating their long-time standard-bearer. Calhoun died soon after, leaving historians to ponder why and how this bitter opponent of Federalism could have made such a profound change of heart.

No historian has ever been able to explain Calhoun's transformation. If one delves deeply enough, however, one comes across an odd incident, generally forgotten, which may go a long way toward explaining the mystery of Calhoun's rejection of secessionism.

One morning in the 1840s, Calhoun and several like-minded congressmen were having breakfast in Washington. Calhoun seemed distracted, gazing strangely at his right hand, nervously trying to brush something off it with his other hand. Finally, his friend Robert Toombs, of Georgia, asked Calhoun what the matter was. Did his hand hurt?

Calhoun at first tried to dismiss the whole thing. It was nothing, he informed his friends, just a bad dream he had the night before that was causing him to imagine a large spot on the back of his right hand. This piqued the curiosity of Toombs and the others even more. They urged him to tell the details of this odd dream. After all, they reassured him, sometimes dreams contain much truth.

Calhoun was not one to divulge his innermost thoughts—much less his dreams—but he was among friends and the vividness of the dream bothered him very much. After some cajoling, Calhoun ventured to tell them of his experience.

The senator had been in his room the night before, writing on a subject dear to his heart—politics. The hour was late, but the topic was an important one, and he was engrossed in his work. Suddenly, a stranger came into the room unannounced. Calhoun was focused on his papers, so he did not hear the door open. The stranger sat down at the table opposite Calhoun without saying a word, as though he belonged there. Calhoun was startled and surprised at the sudden intrusion. Calhoun looked up from his papers to see the man's face, but the stranger had a dark blue cloak, thin and weather-worn, wrapped around him, concealing his features.

The stranger spoke first: "What are you writing, senator from South Carolina?"

The stranger's boldness caught Calhoun off guard, and the senator answered almost automatically, "I am writing a plan for the dissolution of the American Union."

Calhoun, in concert with other like-minded congressmen, had been working on the draft of a scheme for Southern secession—should the need for it arise. It was only a contingency plan at this point, something to threaten the Northern politicians when next they sought to infringe on Southern rights.

The stranger made no comment. Instead, he calmly asked to see Calhoun's right hand. As he extended his hand, the stranger stood up, his cloak parting to reveal underneath the uniform of a general in the old Continental Army. Calhoun gasped when he looked up; for the stranger's face was now uncovered as well, and his features were unmistakable. It was the visage of George Washington, pallid and wraithlike yet quite real. As if in a trance, Calhoun extended his right hand to the apparition. The senator felt a strange tingle as the stranger grasped his hand and held it to the light. After inspecting it, the stranger looked back down at Calhoun and spoke, "Is this the hand, senator, that you would use to sign your name to a declaration dissolving the Union?" he asked. Calhoun replied in the affirmative—if a "certain contingency arose."

With those words a black spot became visible on Senator Calhoun's hand. Disoriented by the event, Calhoun asked what that mark on his right hand was.

"That," said the wraith, "is the mark by which Benedict Arnold is known in the next world."

No sooner had he uttered those words than the apparition drew something from under his cloak and laid it across Calhoun's hands still extended on the table. It was a skeleton.

"These are the bones of Isaac Hayne, hanged at Charleston by the British. He gave his life to establish the Union."

With these words, the stranger left Calhoun's apartment. Shocked at the skeleton being flung at him, the senator from South Carolina awoke with a start—to an empty room.

Had it been just a nightmare, brought on by overwork? Or was it Calhoun's own conscience at work? There is, of course, the other possibility: that the spirit of George Washington—first President of the Union and the man whose whole career was dedicated to its preservation—visited the South's most ardent apologist for States Rights to dissuade him from his course.

Secession would come, of course, in time, but it would not be in the 1840s; and when the time came, it would not be John C. Calhoun's hand that signed any document dissolving the Union.

5

John Brown's Body: Ghosts and Haunts of Harpers Ferry

John Brown's body lies a-mouldering in his grave,
John Brown's body lies a-mouldering in his grave,
John Brown's body lies a-mouldering in his grave,
But his soul goes marching on . . .

Should one sojourn up the Potomac to Harpers Ferry, one cannot fail to come away impressed by the spirit of the place. History comes alive when you visit Harpers Ferry—sometimes quite literally.

Harpers Ferry is best known, of course, for its fatal connection as the site of John Brown's abortive uprising in 1859. But during the War Between the States, Harpers Ferry was much fought over as well. Soldier and civilian alike suffered here during the war, and more than one restless spirit from that era has been reported roaming around the town. But it is of Brown and his followers that the most interesting spectral encounters are known.

John Brown's goals were lofty, even if the means by which he tried to carry them out were base. Brown had concluded some time before, that the institution of slavery would not wither away on its own. The original sin of slavery, he believed, could only be washed away by a baptism of blood. Like the biblical prophets of old, John Brown proposed to smite the Philistine South, hip and thigh, with his own army of the righteous. To this purpose, John Brown would gather up his own latter-day Gideon's Army. To his own clan of close relatives and militant abolitionists, he would add a mighty host of slaves whom he would liberate and arm. He had only to sound the ram's horn in the mountains, he thought, and they would rise up and gather around him as the children of Israel flocked to King David of old—or so Brown fancied.

At first glance, Harpers Ferry was an unlikely spot for a slave revolt. This was not cotton country; most of the surrounding farms were owned by small dirt farmers who owned few, if any, slaves. The town of Harpers Ferry itself held mostly factory or government workers, and ironically nearly half of the town's population of twenty-five hundred were black freemen.

But Harpers Ferry, at the junction of the Potomac and Shenandoah Rivers, was a major rail and road junction as well. To top it off, the town boasted a munitions factory and a government arsenal. By any standard, it was of utmost strategic importance.

Throughout the summer of 1859, Brown waited for a legion of militant abolitionists to flock to his banner. But as summer turned to fall, he grew impatient; he would take action regardless of his numbers, for he was certain he had Providence on his side. Shortly before midnight on October 16, Brown gathered his small force of twenty-one men, left the farmhouse he had been hiding in, and descended the mountain road to Harpers Ferry. As they approached the railway station, the baggage master, a free black named Haywood Shepherd, came out to see what the commotion was. "Halt!" he cried. A shot rang out in the dark, and the baggage master fell to the ground, dead. He was the first victim of Brown's rebellion.

Brown's small army took several hostages from the surrounding countryside and proceeded to seize the government buildings—the arsenal in particular. The first stage of Brown's plan had succeeded.

John Brown now expected the slaves to rise spontaneously from the surrounding countryside. He had even come prepared with firearms and munitions, as well as thousands of long wooden spears tipped with sharp iron blades for use in equipping hordes of runaway slaves.

But the slaves did not come. Instead, angry white citizens attacked Brown and his followers. They retreated to a stoutly built fire hall—later labeled Brown's Fort—and the mob shot all who dared show their faces. One of Brown's men, a free black named Dangerfield Nubie, was shot down as he tried to escape. The mob mutilated Nubie's body for sport, and then flung the corpse to the hogs in a nearby alley.

By morning, the armed citizens had been joined by a detachment of the U.S. Marines under the command of Lt. Col. Robert E. Lee. When the marines assaulted Brown's makeshift fort, it took only three minutes to quash the rebellion.

In due course, Brown and his surviving followers were put on trial. The verdict was a foregone conclusion, but Brown turned the trial into a political platform for his ideas. Bound in a stretcher throughout the proceedings due to his wounds, Brown's oratorical talents came to the forefront. Instead of addressing his treason, Brown put slavery itself on trial, and the nation as a whole for tolerating it. The world could condemn him if it chose, but he would condemn them for their "wicked, cruel, and unjust enactments."

The wind was blowing from the south the day they led John Brown to the place of execution. He mounted the thirteen steps of the gallows not like a condemned criminal but more like Moses ascending the mountain to receive the Law directly from God.

Madman, political incendiary, or martyred saint, take your pick; John Brown was called all of these. Brown was also a man possessed of a ferocious will and singleness of purpose. Certainly mere death could not diminish such a spirit, and he left the world most definitely with "unfinished business."

Among those experts who have studied psychic phenomena, there is general agreement that, while the spirits of most folk pass beyond this world, those who suffer violent deaths or die with earthly concerns still unresolved, often remain bound to this earthly plane as ghosts. And the most likely place for them to haunt is the scene of their most intense emotional trauma before death.

And so it is with Harpers Ferry, the scene of John Brown's moment of glory and defeat, where two of his sons were struck down before his eyes, and where his dreams of liberation were aborted.

There have been a number of ghost sightings in the town of Harpers Ferry for many years now. Many of the witnesses have been tourists, totally unaware of the town's spectral reputation. One incident, in particular, stands out.

One day in the summer of 1974, visitors to Harpers Ferry were in for an unexpected treat. Shirley Dougherty was running a restaurant in town that summer and remembered the visitors coming in and commenting about the "John Brown reenactor" putting on a realistic performance down near the "fort," the site of Brown's last stand.

Apparently, a tall gaunt figure, dressed in old-fashioned clothing, with a wild look in his eyes and a shock of bristly white hair, was wandering near the fort. The Civil War buffs recognized him from old photos as a dead ringer for Brown, looking much as he did at the time of the raid.

Many folks commented to Shirley Dougherty on the reenactor's authentic costume and realistic makeup. What a clever idea for the national park people to stage it, they said. Some even had their photos taken with the man, whom they assumed was re-creating the historic scene. Dougherty was somewhat bewildered because she knew the National Park Service had no such program, nor did the local history association. Who was this man? When the tourists developed their photos, they found that everyone came out except for Brown; they were there, but the man was missing. Five or six such photos were sent to the local National Park Service office with a note describing the incident.

In another incident, a visitor decided to take a stroll by the historic fire-house on a moonlit night. It was the evening of October 16, the anniversary of the raid. Hearing voices coming from within the old building, he came closer—too close. Allegedly, this visitor came face to face with several men dressed in 1850s garb and found himself staring down the barrel of some very real-looking—loaded—muskets. An older man with an intense, piercing gaze began to interrogate him. The terrified visitor fled, the sound of gunfire exploding behind him. He didn't stop until he was back in his own room.

If John Brown is still hanging around Harpers Ferry, he is not alone. The unlucky phantom of poor Dangerfield Nubie is still around as well. Various folk claim to have seen Nubie walking down Hog Alley. On several occasions, even park employees passing the alley late at night have also run into him.

Then too, in nearby St. Peter's Catholic Church, parishioners have observed a visiting priest come and go in a unique manner—right through the walls. They have also heard the wail of a phantom infant on the stone steps of the church. Both apparitions are thought to be civilian victims of an artillery bombardment during the war.

Another Civil War phantom, Jacob, haunts a building that housed a tintype studio during the war. The upper story at that time was also used as a prison for Confederate soldiers. One night Jacob, a Union guard, left his post for a tryst with a local girl. The officer on duty discovered him absent and punished his whole unit for his dereliction.

To get even, Jacob's comrades bound and gagged him. The bashing went too far, however, and Jacob choked to death. The soldiers tried to cover their crime by burying him in secret, dragging his body down the steps, and even dropping him once or twice on the stairwell. Since then, Jacob has made his presence known in various ways. Sounds of the gagging and beating can sometimes be heard inside, as can the loud thumping noise of something heavy being dragged down the stairs. One morning, the letter J was even found engraved on one of the building's windows. Why and how remain a mystery.

To gauge by these and other sightings in and around the town, it would seem that, while his body still lies mouldering, John Brown's soul—and those of quite a few others—still goes marching on in Harpers Ferry.

For information on visiting write the local parks office at Harpers Ferry National Historical Park, P.O. Box 65, Harpers Ferry, WV 25425.

For dedicated ghost hunters, however, it is recommended to take the ghost tour of the town, one of the oldest Civil War ghost tours in the nation. Write or call Ghost Tours of Harpers Ferry, Route 1, Box 468, Harpers Ferry, WV 25425, (304) 725-8019.

6

OOLA AND THE WAR COMET

As the clouds of war loomed larger, signs and portents increased in number and frequency. The last and greatest of these before the actual outbreak of armed conflict was the War Comet.

For centuries comets have been thought to presage great catastrophes both natural and man-made. The comet that appeared over Washington, D.C., in 1861 was no different.

As one by one the Southern states declared their independence and the situation in Charleston Harbor became more critical, the comet arched overhead, an ominous harbinger of imminent doom.

It was, at this point, not at all certain there would be war. The Southern states, arguing that they were within their constitutional rights, hoped to depart the Union peaceably. The Lincoln administration, having called on the states to provide an army of eighty thousand men to suppress the rebellion, hoped that the mere threat of force would be sufficient to restore order.

Despite the gathering clouds of conflict, there were many who still clung to the hope that a compromise would somehow be reached. In the midst of all this, arrived the comet.

As people gazed up in awe at the great comet in the sky, many shuddered with fear of what the future held. The African-American population of Washington, in particular, took the comet quite seriously as an evil omen.

There was residing in the city at this time an ancient black woman, named Oola. She was the slave of the Woodward family. Oola was of pure African blood and possessed of an imposing presence. She was a big woman, and tall, and the wrinkled features of her face seemed like carved ebony, with tufts of white wool springing from her skull in abundance. Her eyes were hawk-like, and when she looked at you, it made you wince—as if a needle had pierced your skull.

All the other servants of the Woodward household—and the black community at large—were terrified of Oola. She had the Evil Eye, they said, and could 'conjure spells.' In the neighborhood where she resided, a number of the children had their fortunes told by Oola; as a rule, whatever Oola predicted, came true, sooner or later. As one of her visitors later observed, having their fortunes told by Oola was, "a terrifying yet fascinating experience."

"You see dat great fire sword blazin' in de sky?" she asked the Taft children one day. "Dat's a great war comin' and de handle's to'rd de Norf and de point to'rd de Souf and de Norf's gwine take dat sword and cut de Souf's heart out. But dat Linkum man, chilluns, if he take de sword, he's gwine perish by it."

Julia Taft, whose brothers were playmates of the Lincoln boys, told Tad Lincoln about the prophecy—omitting, however, the part about his father dying by the sword. Tad was enormously impressed by the story and ran to his father with it. When Tad told him, Lincoln laughed at the tale, but the president was interested in it nonetheless. A few evenings later, he was observed deep in thought, looking out the White House window and peering intently at the War Comet.

Oola, it seems, told true.

PART TWO
SOWING THE WIND: THE BLOODLETTING BEGINS

The war began with many illusions on both sides—that it would all be over in three months, that the other side was just bluffing, that victory could come without a cost, that war was an honorable enterprise waged by gentlemen. These illusions and more would go up in smoke in the course of the first year of the war.

As the war grew in intensity, people took note of various presentments. Even in the early days, strange and unusual events had begun to occur. And as the bloodletting increased, and people became absorbed with the crises before them, less note was taken of such things. Over time, the supernatural effects of these traumatic events became more and more apparent.

7

THE SUNDERED BANNER

The raising of a new flag over the White House has always been an important ceremony, the flag being a symbol of the nation as a whole. In times of war, it takes on added significance.

During the spring of 1861, the war of words between North and South had rapidly escalated into a shooting war. Fort Sumter had fallen to the Rebels at the end of April, and in May first blood had been shed—that of the dashing Colonel Ellsworth of the Zouaves—in a raid on Alexandria, Virginia.

In sympathy with South Carolina, other Southern states were also declaring their independence—nine all told—and beginning to form a confederation. If prospects were fading for a peaceful resolution to the conflict, Lincoln's administration was still hopeful that the rebellion could be quelled with only minimal loss of life and the Union preserved intact. It is against this background, that the incident of June 29, 1861, must be viewed.

A dazzling array of officials were gathered that day on the south portico of the White House. Clusters of generals and their aides, members of the cabinet, and a gaggle of gossiping females, resplendent in hoopskirts and blossoming bonnets, were all gathered to watch the tall, spare form of the President raise the new flag over the nations capitol. The moment came for the flag to be raised, and the marine band began to play the national anthem. Everyone stood, the officers saluting, the civilians taking off their hats. But when the president pulled on the cord, it stuck. Lincoln pulled harder on the rope, but still the flag refused to budge.

One does not split rails for a living without developing some power in one's arms, and old Abe finally gave the line a good strong tug. Suddenly, the upper corner of the flag tore off and hung down in front of him. An audible gasp of horror and surprise arose from those gathered around the president. This sinister omen needed no interpretation.

For a moment, everyone was stunned. Then, with great presence of mind, a young staff officer quickstepped over to the ladies, held out his hands, and hissed, "Pins! Pins!" His pleas did not go unheeded. Mrs. Lincoln and the other women contributed several small barbs, taking them from various hiding places on their persons.

In short order, the Union officer pinned the wayward constellation of stars back together with those stars of the Union blue that had not separated from the flag, and the sundered banner was made whole again. The president raised the flag without further incident.

Down below, the crowd on the lawn, gathered to watch the ceremony, was unaware of the brief but frantic scene around the flagpole. The band had continued to play, and the public was only aware of a slight delay in the ceremony. To the senior administration officials who witnessed the event, however, it was a rather serious matter. Judge Taft, in charge of the Patent Office at the time, warned his teenage daughter not to breathe a word of what she had witnessed. "It will be suppressed," he declared. And so it was. For many years, this supposedly minor incident remained a dark secret, hidden from the world, and known but to a few.

One observer of the flag-raising, a reporter for a local paper, was ignorant of the malign omen, yet even from a distance he noticed that a strange look came over Lincoln's face. He described the president as having "abstract and serious eyes which seemed withdrawn into an inner sanctuary." General Banks, also present, was likewise "much disturbed."

Was it mere chance, a random accident with no further meaning? At this distance in time, the cynic might easily argue that point. Today, for example, the order of the stars in the Union field of the flag represents their order of admission to the Union. From that perspective, the sundering of the nine would have had no significance. But this ordering of the stars is of modern origin; prior to 1912, there was no such rule. Moreover, the men who witnessed the incident were by no means a superstitious lot. They were hard-headed politicians and pragmatic military men.

Yet, all there immediately saw the symbolism inherent in the random accident. Lincoln, attempting to raise the flag on high, had inadvertently torn the Union apart; and now it was only re-joined through direct military intervention.

For some seventy years word of the incident was indeed suppressed, and all the men and women who witnessed it, save one, took the secret with them to their graves.

Coincidence or uncanny omen? It all depends on your point of view.

8

JULIA GRANT'S
SINGULAR VISION

When Sam Grant married Julia Dent, he knew she was a lady of great beauty and rare talents. Captain Grant had little inkling, however, just how rare some of those talents were. Even before the outbreak of the war, Julia Grant demonstrated a knack for having presentments that would invariably come true.

The daughter of a Missouri planter, Julia and her captain resided for a time in St. Louis, near her family. They lived happily in Missouri, Sam Grant having a talent for farming. In 1854, however, at the urging of Grant's father, they traveled to Kentucky to visit his family and pursue the prospect of working in the family business.

It was a sunny day when they arrived, yet no sooner had they stepped off the steamboat than a dark cloud obscured the morning sun. "I hope this is not ominous of our visit," Julia said. Her "Ulys" was quick to reassure her, but in fact, her woman's intuition was correct. The visit to Grant's Kentucky relations was an unpleasant experience for them both. A dark cloud had, in fact, temporarily overshadowed their sunny marriage.

Julia experienced other incidents; individually they were minor in nature, but collectively they were indicative of Julia having some psychic ability. But it was not until the war broke out and her beloved Ulys was exposed to mortal danger that these abilities came to the forefront.

While the federal government initially snubbed Ulysses S. Grant's offers of service, the state of Illinois was not so reluctant. Helping to organize the initial levy of state militia troops called up for active service, Grant was given command of the Twenty-first Illinois Infantry and was soon promoted to brigadier by the governor.

Early on in the conflict, Grant was given orders to make a demonstration across the river in Missouri. Historians refer to the ensuing affair as the Battle of Belmont, although the raid had more the air of a school-yard scrap, than a serious pitched battle. Still, the Battle of Belmont was a deadly enough encounter. Grant had debarked some twenty-five hundred men from river steamboats to break up a concentration of Confederates that had been assembling in the vicinity of Belmont and to divert attention away from hard-pressed pro-Union troops elsewhere in Missouri.

Both sides in the battle were green, not used to combat or military discipline. The Union troops, however, had the benefit of Grant's leadership, and without too much difficulty they defeated the Confederate force and took their camp.

The trouble began when the Union troops began looting the Rebel camp. The prospect of all that booty made the troops—officers included—forget all the enemy still about them. No manner of threats or commands by Grant could get his officers and men to forgo their looting and pursue the enemy.

While Grant's men were busy with booty, the Confederates had time to regroup, work their way behind the Union troops, and cut them off from their boats. Surrounded, Grant's men suddenly realized the danger they were in. His officers were all for surrendering, but Grant was adamant. "We plowed our way through, and we can plow our way back," he said. Sure enough, a determined charge dispersed the Rebel troops and cleared the route back to the boats.

Meanwhile, Rebel reinforcements were seen approaching in the distance. So, while his men made their way onto the boats, Grant rode off to one side to see how close the new Rebel troops were. He had not gone far when he observed gray-clad columns advancing a few dozen yards away. Turning around, he spurred his horse, barely escaping a hail of bullets. The general made a wild ride toward the riverbank, bullets whistling past his ears all the while.

Reaching the river, Grant found his entire command already embarked, the paddle-wheeler in the process of pulling into midstream. Luckily, the boat captain halted the steamer and extended a gangplank. Grant galloped down the riverbank and into the water and, fine horseman that he was, managed to charge right up the narrow plank, still mounted on his horse, ending up on the deck of the boat.

This incident was the closest Grant ever came to death during the course of the war. That same day, far away in Galena, Illinois, Julia was making preparations to join her husband in the field. In the middle of the afternoon, she started becoming very nervous and was unable to go on with packing. She excused herself from the chore, and went to her room to rest for a few moments.

When Julia entered her room, she distinctly saw "Ulys" a few yards distant from her. There, she distinctly saw Ulys a few yards away. She could only see his head and shoulders, and he seemed elevated, as if on horseback. The vision of her husband was so lucid and so real that, startled, Julia called his name out loud.

A friend rushed into the room to see what was wrong. When Julia told her friend of the vision, she dismissed it as nervousness. That evening, Julia and her children left by train for Grant's headquarters in Illinois, but before leaving, Julia received word of the Battle of Belmont.

Grant was waiting for the train when it pulled into Cairo, Illinois. Julia told the general of her seeing him on the day of the battle. Grant asked Julia what time of the day it was that her vision occurred.

When she told him, Grant said, "That is singular. Just about that time, I was on horseback and in great peril, and I thought of you and the children. I was thinking of you, my dear Julia, and very earnestly too."

It was indeed a most singular vision, but it would not be Julia Grant's last by any means.

9

SMOOT'S GHOST

When the autumn days turn crisp, the nights frosty, and the shadows grow long upon the land, folks along the Tennessee border get to talking about the old days. One of the tales they tell is the story of Smoot's ghost.

In 1820, the Wheatley family founded its farm, named Oaklands, in the northern part of Montgomery County, Tennessee, just below the Kentucky border. A few years before the war a man named John Walton Barker bought Oaklands Plantation from the Wheatleys. Barker, busy with other ventures, soon hired a man to run the place—a man named Smoot.

By all accounts, Smoot was a most conscientious overseer. He was hard working and honest, and he drove his field hands no harder than he drove himself. He never married, though, and running a farm can be a lonely life for a man like him. Aside from the slaves and the hogs, Smoot had little company, and no close friends.

When the war broke out in 1861, nothing changed much at first. The soil still needed tilling, the tobacco still needed curing, and the hogs, it seemed, needed to be fed just about constantly. But in February 1862, when the Yankees took Forts Donelson and Henry downriver and occupied nearby Clarksville, the situation changed. Slave from Oaklands ran off to be "contraband" with the Union army, leaving old Smoot to run the farm by himself. Now his only company was the hogs.

Old Smoot did the best he could to run the farm alone, including slopping the hogs, but the going was not easy. And what with the Yankee patrols and local guerrilla bands, it could be downright dangerous at times.

Neighboring farmers did not see Smoot every day, so at first no one was unduly alarmed about his welfare when he did not come to town on market day as usual. When a week or so passed, however, and no one had seen hide nor hair of old Smoot, the neighbor folk decided to mosey on over to Oaklands to see if he was alright.

Riding up to Oaklands, the men were puzzled. On first glance, everything seemed in order. The house and outbuildings looked well kept, and the hogs out back seemed well fed. But repeated calls of Smoot's name brought no response. The men dismounted and fanned out in search of the overseer. As they crossed the farmyard, a few of the men noted how active the hogs seemed—uncommonly active. Snorting and snuffling with particular gusto, the porkers were engrossed in a feast of some magnitude. That was odd, for how could the hogs be eating if no one was around to feed them?

The frenzy with which the hogs were gorging themselves was downright unnerving. Curious, a few of the men walked over to investigate. Peering over the split rails of the pen, the neighbors solved the mystery but wished they hadn't. They had found Smoot—or rather, what was left of him.

After they extracted Smoot's mangled remains from the pen of frenzied swine, they gave his gnawed and gnarled flesh as decent a burial as they could. The mystery remained, however. What had caused Smoot's demise? If he died of natural causes, how did he end up in the hog pen? If not, then who did it and why?

Marion Henry Hamner, for one, was always certain of the answer. The great-granddaughter of the plantation owner, John Barker, she grew up on Oaklands Plantation. Mrs. Hamner was always of the opinion that the Yankees were to blame for Smoot's death.

During the Late Unpleasantness, "Yankee" and "thief" were more or less synonymous, at least in that part of the country. Federal foraging parties out of Clarksville constantly combed the countryside, requisitioning livestock for the Union army and commandeering whatever property they thought fit from hapless farmers.

The Yankee patrols were supposed to give civilians script for anything they took. In actual fact, the foragers—"bummers"—were rarely so particular, and if anyone objected too much, they were paid in hot lead.

Mrs. Hamner had no doubt that old Smoot, conscientious to the last, protested the seizure of some plantation plow-horses or the contents of the corn-crib and was cut down by the invaders in blue. Adding insult to deadly injury, they dumped his body in the hog pen to be devoured by the swine, and perhaps to cover up evidence of their crime.

The full story of Smoot's death may never be known. But whatever the truth of the matter, no one in Montgomery County doubts that ever since his grisly demise, strange things have been seen and heard at Oaklands Plantation. For while Smoot's remains were laid to rest, his spirit was not.

On certain nights of the year, folks have seen eerie lights flickering about Oaklands. On those nights, the weird light can be seen moving to and fro, bobbing about and looking very much like a lantern held aloft.

A number of the residents of Peacher's Mill Road, where Oaklands lies, as well as casual passersby have seen this spectral light on the plantation. The folks in that neck of the woods will tell you that it's old Smoot, still making the early morning rounds on the farm.

Mrs. Hamner and some neighboring folk have also heard strange noises in the pen, and have seen the flickering light move between the Oaklands family graveyard and the site of the old Wheatley Mill.

While Mrs. Hamner has never seen old Smoot herself, on many occasions she has heard his voice calling. Weird sounds emanate from the hog pen where he died, as well.

All this is, admittedly, most strange; but on Peacher's Mill Road, up along the Kentucky border, it's all par for the course. Smoot is one of several phantoms that haunt the neighborhood. As for Smoot, it is said he will never rest until he is laid whole in his grave. In which case, Smoot will be with us for a long, long time.

10

THE HEADLESS PHANTOM
OF CEDAR LANE

Before the war, the Montgomery House was a resplendent mansion along a rural lane on the outskirts of Nashville. It had originally been the residence of Mrs. Alexander B. Montgomery, a prominent citizen and loyal daughter of the South.

Mrs. Montgomery stayed in her mansion on Cedar Lane for many years, next to what is now the cosmopolitan neighborhood of Belmont. According to one old Confederate veteran, she continued to reside there, in fact, long after she died. She could not leave, it was said, because she had a treasure to protect.

Soon after the Yankees seized Forts Donelson and Henry on the Tennessee and Cumberland Rivers and occupied Clarksville, Grant's forces quickly moved upstream and seized Nashville—the Confederates having abandoned it without a shot.

Many of the local population panicked and fled at the news of the Yankee army's approach, but not Mrs. Montgomery. This belle was a confirmed Rebel, and she would not be so easily moved. She resolved to make her stand, come what may.

One day, however, there was a loud banging on the front door. Yankee officers from the provost marshal's office announced that, by order of the military governor, Montgomery House would be turned into a hospital. Mrs. Montgomery was ordered to vacate the premises within twenty-four hours.

Rather than let the Yankees have her ancestral home and liberty to loot it at will—not to mention providing aid and comfort to the enemy—Mrs. Montgomery stripped the house of all its belongings and buried the family silver and other valuables in the rose garden. This done, she then set fire to her home.

After freeing her slaves, Mrs. Montgomery then set out along the Natchez Trace with whatever she could carry with her. Unfortunately, as she was crossing over the no-man's land separating the two contending armies, she was caught in a brief but bitter skirmish. In the midst of the fray, she was beheaded by a stray cannonball.

Now, local legend held that since that terrible day, the spirit of Mrs. Alexander Montgomery was unable to get away from her ancestral home, charred shell though it may have been. From time to time, passersby see a headless specter wandering the grounds and outbuildings of the Montgomery place. She haunts the grounds, they say, because she is guarding treasure buried somewhere on the property.

Legends of restless revenants and buried treasure abound, especially in the South. One is tempted to dismiss the headless phantom of Cedar Lane as just another fable. But some years back, some local good old boys resolved to test the old legend and see for themselves if the headless belle was indeed guarding a buried hoard. On a dark night, they crept with shovel and pick onto the little lane off Belmont Boulevard. The rose garden was now a tangle of thorns and thistles, where it once had been a neatly tended formal garden. With one eye out for a headless guardian spirit, the men dug and dug. Finally, to their surprise, they hit something solid. In the dim light of their oil lamps, the white glint of metal shone from the ground. They had indeed found a cache of silver coins, serving spoons, and other items that had once been the domestic service of Mrs. Montgomery. The men kept quiet about their find and sold most of it for cash. But a few pieces, kept as souvenirs and handed down to their children, remain as physical evidence to the veracity of the tales told about the old Montgomery place.

Once the treasure was exposed to the light of day, the spirit of its former owner was freed from her guardianship of it. She has never been sighted since. Today, there survive only a few serving spoons as proof of the truth of the headless phantom of Cedar Lane.

11

THE PHANTOM DRUMMER OF SHILOH

Though foreign to modern sensibility, prior to the Civil War, it was common to find children hard at work in the fields and factories of America. When the war came, many youths, motivated by a yearning for adventure and glory, volunteered for service on both sides. So long as they looked old enough, recruiters were inclined to turn a blind eye to their age. Boys too young or too small to pass muster, could still hope to be taken on as a drummer boy or bugler.

Though considered non-combatants, the drummer boy was exposed to as much danger—maybe more— than the average soldier. Out in front of the line, so that his drum-rolls could be heard, with the man who bore the flag, the drummer was often more exposed to fire than the rest of the regiment.

These young boys were renowned for their courage—the most famous being Johnny Clem, called variously Johnny Shiloh, or the "Drummer Boy of Chickamauga." A drummer for the Union side, his exploits on the battlefield won him fame and a promotion to regular service.

The story of Johnny Clem ought not to be confused with that of the Drummer Boy of Shiloh. This latter hero remains anonymous, and most historians have relegated him to the status of legend. Folks say this drummer boy still lingers on Shiloh's placid fields.

Who was the phantom drummer, and why does he haunt those green fields so far from home?

To delve into the truth of the matter, one must go back to the fateful days of early April 1862. It is not generally recounted, but there were, in fact, two battles of Shiloh fought back to back. The first was fought by Grant's Army of the Tennessee—a battle that Grant lost. The succeeding fight was won by Gen. Don Carlos Buell's Army of the Ohio the next day.

Early on April 6, the Army of the Tennessee was sleeping peacefully in their tents when a surprise assault was launched by a massive combined force of Confederates under Gen. Albert Sidney Johnston. In the ensuing rout, Grant's army was nearly annihilated. Grant himself—hung over, some say—did not appear on the battlefield for several hours after it had begun.

It was only a massed barrage of heavy artillery that halted the Confederate onslaught. Grant's army had been pushed back to a small toehold around the steamboat dock at Pittsburg Landing. By any definition of the term, Grant's was a defeated army.

Luckily, Buell's fifty-five thousand-man Army of the Ohio had arrived on the other bank of the Tennessee River after a 122-mile march from Nashville. As soon as they were ferried across the river, Buell's undefeated troops went into the line at Shiloh, bolstering the shattered remnants of Grant's command. What Buell's men saw as they arrived was not so much an army as a terror-stricken mob. Ten thousand or more men, leaderless and broken, were huddled around the landing in a pouring rain. Many preferred to take a bullet in the head for deserting than go back into the line of battle.

But as a new day dawned, Buell's midwesterners turned defeat into victory. They counterattacked, driving the depleted Rebel troops back over the blood-soaked ground.

It was on this second day of battle, the second Shiloh, that a drummer boy with one of Buell's regiments was ordered to sound the drumroll, "Attack." The young boy, the drum nearly dwarfing his small frame, grabbed his drumsticks and dutifully obeyed. In response, a cohort of blue-clad men moved forward as one, left feet first, lines properly dressed and marching forward with neat precision, just as they had been drilled so many times before in camp. With bayonets fixed and muskets primed and loaded, the regiment advanced on a crucial Confederate position near Shiloh Church. But as they neared the position, resistance increased, and the Federals became stalled on the side of a slope. Over the din of battle, the officer yelled to the drummer boy to sound the drumroll for "Retreat."

The boy hesitated a second, then picked up his sticks again and began to beat out a call—"Attack." The officer bellowed at the poor boy. Had he not heard the order to sound a retreat?

"Indeed, sir," pleaded the boy, "but 'Attack' is all I know! I never learned 'Retreat'!"

By now it was too late to recall the men. To the wonder of the officer, the well-trained regiment had resumed their advance, charging uphill despite the withering fire from the heights above. To everyone's surprise, the regiment reached the Confederate position and after a short, sharp fight, drove the Rebels back. With that commanding height in place, the course of battle turned in favor of the Federals.

When the smoke cleared and the regiment re-formed, the commander sought out the drummer boy to commend him. He found the youth; the boy lay dead upon the hillside, drumsticks still in hand, with his drum beside him and a bullet through his heart.

Historians today may scoff at the tale, but it is a tradition handed down from the time of the battle, and there is testimony that tends to corroborate the story.

During the 1940s, a construction crew putting in a new road through the park, uncovered a body. At that time, the person overseeing the park was a man named Captain Rice. A journalist visiting Rice about this time had happened to inquire about the legend of the Drummer Boy of Shiloh, and in answer to the question, Rice showed him the remains.

Smaller than an adult skeleton, there was no question that it had once been a child. Most organic matter had long since rotted—flesh, clothing, and wooden drum. But around its neck were pieces of the drum cord and a lead bullet, lodged in its chest where the heart had once been. Captain Rice never made the find public, but he and the journalist were convinced it was proof of the legend.

Every legend, they say, has its basis in fact. And if the Drummer Boy's story be true, then the other half of the tale is credible as well. For decades, visitors to Shiloh in the spring have, from time to time, heard the distant roll of a drum, the staccato beats wafting on soft spring air.

It adds to the realism of the battlefield, visitors have said, complimenting the staff on such a neat little touch. But no such enhancement has ever been authorized by the tours, and the reenactors do not normally encamp there so early in the season. Those who know say it is the phantom drummer boy dutifully thumping away on his drum, calling forth a spectral army to the attack.

Across the open fields, sounds of phantom drums and ghostly gunfire are still heard on occassion. Only a few have actually experienced it, but those who have heard the sound of the Phantom Drummer Boy are certain of what they heard.

The Phantom Drummer Boy is not the only spectral phenomenon observed at Shiloh, to be sure. They are all indications to us that, if memory of the horror of Shiloh has long since faded from the living, for the dead it is still a most vivid and current event, a memory that rumbles through the halls of eternity like a distant drumroll.

12

MRS. WALLACE'S
PRESENTMENT

It was formerly a widespread belief—and is still current in some quarters—that marriage is not just a physical union, but a spiritual one too. By this notion, the wedding of a man and wife is not simply the joining of the flesh, but a melding of souls, as well. Though the two be separated physically, the two souls remain as one and remain in communion on some plane, even if there be no direct material contact. Thus, one hears of reports of spouses, widely separated in space, sensing their mate's thoughts or feelings, particularly when they are exposed to mortal danger.

Likewise, there are also cases where the spouse, even before an event of great hazard has occurred, has foreknowledge—a presentment they used to call it—of something dangerous yet to come. In wartime, this is a particularly noteworthy event.

Although science refuses to recognize such things as intuition or premonition, it remains the most widely experienced of paranormal phenomena. During the Civil War, we have a number of such incidents documented; such is the case with Mrs.Wallace.

One of the more able Union generals in the Western Theater of War was Major-General W. H. L. Wallace. A competent divisional commander under Grant, he was highly regarded by both his men and the Lincoln administration.

Before the war, Wallace had been a lawyer, active in Illinois politics. When war broke out, Wallace, seeking to help his friend and former associate, Abraham Lincoln, was given command of the Eleventh Illinois Infantry. His leadership ability soon brought him promotion, first to brigadier, then to major-general in command of one of the six divisions in Grant's Army of the Tennessee. March of 1862 found Wallace's division encamped with the rest of the army near the crude wooden church called Shiloh.

Ann Wallace had watched her husband march off to war with mixed emotions. Riding at the head of a column of men, he looked grand in his new blue uniform. She was proud that her William was helping Lincoln save the Union, but she was also apprehensive. Although everyone said the war would be over in a few weeks, she sensed that the struggle would be much longer and that her William would be exposed to far more danger than anyone imagined. Certainly, Ann Wallace shared these and many other concerns with fellow army wives whose husbands had also marched off to war. But at the beginning of spring 1862, an overwhelming sense of foreboding crept over Ann. She could not put her finger on any rational reason why she should feel this way; but there was no denying it either. As April approached, Mrs. Wallace became haunted with an impression of impending doom, until she could stand it no longer.

With an urgency in her that she could not explain, Ann left to join her husband as a "surprise." In one of the most severe storms of that year, at the stroke of midnight, Ann Wallace started out alone for the army where her husband was serving.

Going downriver to Cairo, Ann tried to take a ship up the Tennessee River. She was flat-out refused, being told that no women were permitted beyond that point. Most of the journey was through hostile territory, with roving bands of guerrillas poised to attack at any moment.

As one family friend noted, "Affection has a persistency that will not be denied." The general's wife ran into a delegation from their hometown of Ottawa, Illinois. They were headed upstream to present a new flag to the Eleventh Illinois—the general's old regiment—the unit's old standard having been worn out by hard campaigning.

Ann persuaded the color guard to allow her to bear the new colors to the regiment. Using this flag as her shield, she successfully dodged hostile forces—not just the Confederates, but the far more hostile forces of the Union's provost guards.

Arriving on the shore opposite Pittsburg, landing on a dark and stormy night, Ann found out how true her premonition was. A ferocious battle was being fought on the opposite shore, and somewhere in that hell was her poor husband. It was a night of terror and dismay; half of Grant's army was dead, captured, or fled. Panic-stricken soldiers preferred drowning to facing the enemy again, and it seemed that death awaited anyone who ventured across those Stygian waters to the far shore.

But Ann had come this far, and she would not turn back now, no matter what horrors she witnessed. She had to be with her husband, come what may. That night, as a regiment of Buell's rescue force was ferried over, a noncom with the Ninth Indiana recalled seeing her on the bridge of the steamboat that ferried them across. She peered intently into the darkness as if she could see through the dark to where the men lay on the battlefield.

When Ann reached the far shore, all was chaos. Men by the thousands crowded the dock seeking to escape. The newly arrived troops, Ann sheltering behind them, could only get through by fixing bayonets and forcing a passage up the slopes to the front.

Amid the jumble and confusion, Ann finally found familiar faces. But their words confirmed what her heart had already been telling her; that General Wallace was missing in action and presumed dead. He had rallied some men that afternoon, trying to halt the Rebel onslaught. But that was the last anyone had seen of him. The position had been overrun, everyone now fled, dead, or captured.

The next morning brought a stop to the rain and a ray of hope. When Buell's boys counterattacked, they retook the sunken road called the Hornet's Nest and came across General Wallace. He had been badly wounded, but was alive. Alone, and exposed to a pouring rain, some kindly Confederate had wrapped him in a blanket.

Rushed aboard the steamer, Wallace and his wife were reunited. The steamer took them upstream to Savannah, Tennessee, where Grant had his headquarters. He was placed in an upstairs bedroom in the Cherry Mansion and given the best care available. At first, Wallace responded well to the care, and doctors thought they had gotten to him in time. But his head wound and subsequent exposure overnight had proven too much in the end. As Ann described it, "He faded away like a fire going out." By April 10, William Wallace was dead.

There are those who will dismiss Ann Wallace's presentment with the usual excuse—coincidence. But to the Wallaces and those who knew them, Ann's foreboding and her compulsion to rush to her husband's side were far from coincidental. Clearly, in some manner she sensed her husband was in danger. She arrived too late to change his fate, however. At least though, Ann was able to be with him in the end, to comfort him and let him know how much she loved him still.

There is an interesting supernatural sequel to the paranormal experiences of Ann Wallace. The house William Wallace expired in—Cherry Mansion—is still standing in Savannah, Tennessee. While his body was brought back to Ottowa, Illinois, by all accounts, some part of his essence remains bound to the house he died in.

On occasion, passersby have seen a man staring out from the upstairs bedroom window of the mansion. He is clad in a dark uniform and wears a broad-brimmed hat like the ones officers wore during the Civil War. The general is one of several ghosts known to inhabit Cherry Mansion, and some think he is reliving his final days of life, the days spent with his beloved—and psychic—wife.

13

ANTIETAM: "DECK THE HALLS!"

Mourn ye the blood on this steel rusted blade,
'Tis all that is left of the Irish Brigade.
—Major Lawrence Reynolds

The Battle of Antietam, fought on September 17, 1862, was the bloodiest day in American history. Between sunrise and sunset some twenty-four thousand men were killed, wounded, or captured. The number of casualties at Antietam alone exceeded the total number of dead from all three of the nation's previous wars combined: the American Revolution, the War of 1812, and the Mexican War.

Many were the heroic deeds done that day; many more were the groans of the wounded and dying when the shooting stopped. Farmhouses and churches were overflowing with a mass of casualties, and even then, the wounded overflowed to the surrounding grounds. In the fields, the ground was thick with a newly mown harvest of death.

While much has been written of the many deeds done that day, none was more bold or braver—or more futile—than the charge of the Irish Brigade against the Rebel line at Bloody Lane. In the mid-nineteenth century, large numbers of Irish, like the Germans, came to America in search of a better life and political liberties. Although looked down on by the Anglo-Saxon majority, both groups eagerly flocked to the flag when the Union was threatened with secession in 1861.

Large numbers of Irish volunteered for service with the Sixty-ninth New York Militia. Although only in service a brief time, they acquitted themselves honorably at First Bull Run. The regiment was later reformed along more permanent lines, and then joined with similar units to form the legendary Irish Brigade. When the Confederates under Gen. Robert E. Lee crossed the Potomac River in the late summer of 1862 and invaded Maryland, the Irish Brigade was among those Union forces that marched to stop General Lee's advance.

The dawn of September 17 saw the Army of Northern Virginia on the defensive, holding a line along Antietam Creek near the small community of Sharpsburg. For once, George McClellan, the Union commander, went on the offensive, hurling his huge force against Lee's prepared positions.

By midmorning, the focus of the action had shifted to the center of the line, where General Sumner's Second Corps charged against D. H. Hill's Alabamans and North Carolinians. Although outnumbered by Sumner's Federals, the Southerners had found a strong position: a sunken road running southeast of the Roulette Farm and forming a ready-made trench that faced an open field.

The Irish Brigade was ordered to attack across this field. They had earned a reputation for reckless bravery, and they more than justified it this day. Charging headlong across some 350 yards of flat, featureless ground, the Irish endured a withering fire.

The blue-clad ranks fell by the score, but for nearly four hours the Irish Brigade, emboldened by their weird war cry and their emerald-green banner, pressed their attack, losing 60 percent of their men in the process.

The sunken road the Irish men fought so hard to gain that day earned the name "Bloody Lane" as a result. After the battle, it was said one could walk end to end along the lane without ever touching the ground, so thick was it with corpses.

According to tradition, Lee asked what regiment had led the gallant charge against Bloody Lane. When he was informed it was the Sixty-ninth New York, Lee is reputed to have said, "Ah yes, the Fighting Sixty-ninth." From that day forth, the regiment retained that nickname.

Today, of course, it is hard to imagine that the placid fields and rolling hills which surround the picturesque town of Sharpsburg were the scene of so much carnage. The rural scenery and neatly manicured fields of a national park form a stark contrast to the scene that Stonewall's staff witnessed at twilight on the seventeenth.

By dusk, the sounds of battle had tapered off, only to be replaced by more terrible sounds—the moans and groans of thousands of wounded men. "Pitiable cries for water and pleas for help were much more terrible," Henry Kyd Douglas tells us, "than the deadliest sounds of battle. Silent were the dead and motionless, but here and there were raised stiff arms. Heads made a last effort to lift themselves from the ground. Prayers were mingled with oaths, and midnight hid all distinction between blue and gray."

But that is long vanished now, and the fields are host, not to the dead and dying, but to children and adults curious to see this particular field of glory. Over the years, many school groups have come to visit Antietam National Battlefield, near Sharpsburg, Maryland. For students, it is an edifying and educational experience—a chance to see history "come alive."

For several years running, one such school—the exclusive McDonogh School of Baltimore, Maryland—had routinely visited Antietam on class trips. For the blue-clad boys of the McDonogh School, however, the experience has proved to be more than just an academic exercise. In fact, one seventh grade class even taught a thing or two about the supernatural to its teacher.

One of the teachers, Mr. O'Brien, was quite knowledgeable about American history, and with the aid of local park rangers and volunteer reenactors, he put on a comprehensive tour of the famed battlefield. It was a program which combined history, English, and the social sciences.

Soon after they arrived at the park, the seventh graders would line up in their neat blue blazers and learn the parade drill and the manual of arms. Reenactors would demonstrate how to load and fire a Civil War musket and would give other details of a soldier's life. Then, after lunch, the students would tramp about the battlefield, trying to absorb highlights from the history of the battle.

Toward dusk, the McDonogh boys would end up at Bloody Lane with the zigzag split-rail fence now meticulously restored by the National Park Service. The boys were stationed one to a fence post, allowing them some quiet time to reflect on the day's events.

As they walked back to the buses, O'Brien told them to write an essay about what they had learned and what parts of the visit had impressed them the most. With memory of the visit still fresh in their minds, the boys took out their spiral notebooks, and on the ride back to Baltimore, wrote down their impressions.

The essays were quite varied; some even writing bits of poetry. The Bloody Lane loomed large in their essays, it being the last stop on the tour and freshest in their memories. Then too, the stillness at twilight, it seems, had allowed many of the students to perceive things going on around them, things that their adult chaperones and teachers were oblivious to.

As O'Brien was grading the essays a few days later, he began to notice some curious comments scattered among the papers. Some students mentioned hearing chanting, while others said they heard Christmas carols sung in a foreign tongue.

The boys had not had a chance to talk to each other before writing their papers, so there was no possibility of a practical joke. They had definitely experienced something, but what? As O'Brien compared the accounts, he noticed a common thread. The boys had all heard the "caroling in a foreign language" as they sat along the fence bordering Bloody Lane.

More specificially, those with the most vivid impressions of the caroling or chanting had been posted along the lane between the Anderson Cannon Monument and the War Department Observation Tower.

This, the teacher knew, was the exact segment of the line that the Irish Brigade had made their doomed charge against in 1862. A suspicion of what was going on here—however far-fetched it seemed—began to form in the educator's mind. Students on previous trips had also had unusual experiences at that location—one year, for example, seventh graders wrote of smelling the acrid sulfurous scent of gunpowder along that part of Bloody Lane.

In class, the teacher questioned the boys more closely as to what it was they thought they'd heard. Some said they just heard an unintelligible chanting or cheering. Many, however, said the invisible voices seemed to be repeating the chorus to "Deck the Halls."

Mr. O'Brien asked several students to vocalize the sound for him, as they remembered it. They rendered it to him as "Fa-la-la-lah." The teacher, being something of an expert on the War Between the States and the Battle of Antietam in particular, was thunderstruck at what he heard.

What Mr. O'Brien knew—and what the seventh graders could not possibly have known—was that their chant bore a remarkable resemblance to the Gaelic war cry of the Fighting Sixty-ninth. The war cry of the Irish regiment in English is rendered as "Clear the Way"; but in Gaelic it is "Faugh a Ballagh"—pronounced Fa-a-bah-lah. For an expert steeped in the lore of the Civil War, the parallel was obvious. But no ordinary visitor would have been so well versed—much less a group of seventh graders. In the quiet of the battlefield, sitting before the killing field where 540 men of the Irish Brigade fell before the withering fire of Hill's corps, the students of McDonogh School had heard the war cry of the bold Fenian sons of Erin—a sound not heard there in over 120 years.

The experiences of the seventh graders at Antietam were not an isolated incident, of course. At Pry House, "Burnside Bridge," and nearby St. Paul's Episcopal Church, Civil War specters have been reported repeatedly. Even a local bed and breakfast on the field of battle is reputed to be haunted by restless dead of the Civil War.

While many reliable reports of the supernatural emanate from all over the battlefield of Antietam, the singular experience of the students of McDonogh School remain the most credible account to date. In the "landscape turned red" of Antietam, memory of the valor of the Irish Brigade lingers on—in more ways than one.

PART THREE
THE YEAR OF THE JUBILO
(1863)

The year 1863 was the turning point in the war, although it may not have seemed so at the time. It began with Lincoln's Emancipation Proclamation—which though it did not free all the slaves, did have great moral significance. The twin victories of Vicksburg and Gettysburg, coming as they did within days of each other, meant that the Confederacy had reached and passed its "high tide" and was now on the ebb. Moreover, the Federals gained complete control of the vital Mississippi River.

The course of the conflict had pivoted inexorably in favor of the Union, and it would now be a matter of time— and blood—before the end came for the South. As before, with these changes came signs for those willing to heed them. Then too, such great disturbances on the material plane would inevitably leave their mark on the spiritual plane, and there is still abundant evidence for that as well—for those wishing to see them.

14

WHEN THE ANGELS CAME DOWN TO PLAY

This is the year of Jubilee
Send them angels down.
The Lord has come to set us free,
O, send them angels down.

For generations uncounted, African-Americans had been held in bondage, all the time yearning for the day of their liberation. When the war finally came, to the slaves it seemed as though it were a fulfillment of prophecy. For whatever the war may have been to white folks, to blacks there was no question that it was about slavery and its abolition.

Throughout the South, Lincoln's official proclamation freeing the slaves was greeted with joyous celebration and not a few unusual incidents. With no one present able to record them, many such incidents were soon forgotten. But to those who witnessed them, many could not help but mark them as signs of divine approval for this political act.

It was a dark and stormy night in a part of South Carolina then under Federal control. Whites and blacks were gathering together in a little cabin to listen to the proclamation from the President, officially setting them free. The edict was to take effect at midnight, and as the witching hour approached, a deathly silence prevailed. At the head of a rough board table in the middle of the room, one elderly Negro, named Uncle Ben, possessed a watch and was more or less the official timekeeper for announcing when their hour of liberation had arrived. All eyes were focused at the old man and his watch.

As the appointed time neared, a Yankee soldier in blue had read to them the president's proclamation, and Uncle Ben began counting off the last few seconds before midnight.

"By the time I counts ten," he said, "it will be midnight, and the land will be free: one, two, three, four, five, six, seven, eight, nine. . ."

Just at that moment music started coming from a banjo hanging on the wall, as if to complete the old man's countdown. The sound of the music was loud and distinct, and at the chords resounding in the air, all the blacks as a body fell to their knees and began to pray, the old man leading them:

"Thou did promise that one of thy angels should come and give us the sign, and shore 'nuff, the sign did come. We's grateful oh, we's grateful, O Lord. Send thy angel once more to give that sweet sound!"

No sooner did the words pass across the black elder's lips, than another strain came from the banjo, followed immediately by a flash of lightning and a thunderous boom.

No clearer sign could be asked for, so far as the occupants of the cabin were concerned. They rose to their feet to sing a chorus of their favorite gospel song. After one stanza, they fell on their knees again, and Uncle Ben led them in a fervent and heartfelt prayer of liberation, followed by more singing. And when they were finished, the congregation hugged each other in joy shouting, "Glory, glory to God, we are free!"

As they were in the midst of this, the banjo again played a sweet strain of music as if in final confirmation of the divine presence that had come among them. Uncle Ben proclaimed, "the angels of the Lord is with us still, and they is watching over us, for old Sandy told us more than a month ago that they would."Apparently, someone in the community had predicted both their liberation and the divine sign, well before anyone knew such an event would transpire.

As for Mr. Brown, one of the white men in the cabin, he remained unconvinced of any supernatural agency. He said it was merely "a vibration of the strings caused by the wind" and proceeded to try to impose his views on the congregation. While Ben and the others tried to be as respectful as they could to Mr. Brown, they remained unconvinced by his skepticism, and in fact, went on to cite many other unusual portents in recent days, all of which had served to convince them that something momentous was to occur in their lives. And indeed it had.

The Bible is full of natural events that have a supernatural cast: the sun stands still in the sky and victory is given to the children of Israel; a star appears in the heavens, and three astrologers declare that a child born to a poor family in a small Palestinian village is the King of Kings.

Blacks in the South had looked to the Bible for generations and found in its pages confirmation of their own plight and a promise of their eventual liberation. Now the prophecies, uttered by hundreds of Uncle Bens throughout the South, had come true at last.

The cynics scoffed at such things, or found it a source of mirth; but for those who had been in bondage it was no joke. Of all the times for the wind to play with the strings of the instrument and the lightning and thunder to be loosed, why then?

The minor incident in that cabin in South Carolina was repeated throughout the South; largely though, these omens and signs went unrecorded, unless some outside observers were present to record them.

Interestingly, on more than one occasion, Union soldiers observed as they marched through the South, that the local black population often had foreknowledge of an event, even before their officers were informed. More than one northerner commented on this in their war memoirs. What white northerners were ignorant of, and white Southerners knew but would not speak of, was a thing called Hoodoo.

Then, as now, Hoodoo was widespread in the South, even if few blacks talked openly of it outside their race. An inheritance from Africa, combined at times with some Native American herbal medicine and a smattering of European folk beliefs, Hoodoo was the country cousin of Voodoo, the better known and more formalized magical tradition of New Orleans and the Caribbean.

There was hardly a plantation in the South that did not have at least one person adept at the practice of Hoodoo. Although it mostly consisted of benign folk medicine, many practitioners seemed to possess genuine psychic gifts. So while even sympathetic Northerners may have scoffed at the superstitions of the blacks they encountered as they invaded the Deep South, the truth was—and is—far more complex.

15

PHANTOMS OF FARNSWORTH HOUSE

It began almost by accident. A Rebel raiding party, looking for shoes of all things, ran into a Union patrol. As each side began pouring men into the fight, it quickly escalated into a full-blown battle—the Battle of Gettysburg.

Initially, Union troops at Gettysburg held the ground north and west of the town itself. But as Confederate reinforcements arrived, the Federals were forced east from Seminary Ridge to Cemetery Ridge, even as they retreated south through town. Inevitably, Gettysburg became the scene of house-to-house fighting, with sharpshooters sniping at each other from windows and doorways. Although civilian casualties were light at Gettysburg, the fight still had a traumatic effect on the town and its people. Physical evidence of the battle remains to this day in the town, visible to the naked eye. Less obvious, but equally substantial, are the supernatural scars that linger from the great battle fought there.

A number of spots throughout the town of Gettysburg have proven to resonate with psychic impressions of that battle. Perhaps the best documented place in Gettysburg with such phenomena is Farnsworth House.

In recent years, this historic home—now a cozy bed and breakfast—has been investigated by several experts in the paranormal. It has also been the subject of several television documentary shows, such as "Sightings" and "The Unexplained." Built around 1810, it was originally a simple two-story wood-frame house. Around 1837, a brick Federal-style wing was added to it. By the time of the Civil War, the Sweeney family occupied it; Catherine Sweeney and her daughter Lizzie lived there during the battle.

The current manager of Farnsworth House, Patty O'Day, knows as much about the spectral residents of Farnsworth and Gettysburg as anyone. But when she and her family moved into the old home, it was solely with the idea of living there. They had no notion of making it a popular tourist attraction, much less any inkling the old place was haunted.

However, like her grandmother before her, Patty soon found she was naturally sensitive to the paranormal. It was not long before she became aware that she and her family were not the only ones residing at Farnsworth House. Farnsworth was host to a number of ghosts.

A few years ago, a skilled psychic, Carol Kirkpatrick, visited the place and gave the O'Day family a "reading" of the house. Her comments confirmed many of their own experiences in the place. For example, over the years, many people have heard the sound of heavy footsteps overhead. They seemed to come from the garret in the brick wing. The door leading up to the garret was always locked, so no living person could have made the sounds. Carol said she felt the presence of three men—Confederate soldiers—in the garret.

In her mind's eye, she could make out one of the men in the garret—a tall, thin fellow with blonde hair. She also supplied a name—George Sutton III. Oddly, she noted that his shoes had a red substance on them. It turns out that on the first day of the battle, Dole's Georgia Brigade had occupied the town, and their sharpshooters had taken up various positions in the homes around town from which to snipe at the Yankees. The "red stuff" she had seen was the red clay of Georgia.

Patty's own research confirmed Carol's discovery. There was indeed a George Sutton III; according to official records, he was from Savannah, had fought at Gettysburg, and had in fact been taken prisoner and sent to the POW camp at Fort McHenry in Maryland.

The garret definitely seems to be a focus of activity at Farnsworth House. In addition to footsteps, the sound of heavy objects being moved has also been heard up there; even the sound of a Jew's harp has occasionally been noted emanating from that same room. One guest in a room directly beneath it heard the soldiers talking one night; the visitor even struck up a conversation with him; the soldier explained to the guest that he was in the garret because he had been ordered to stay at his post—apparently throughout eternity!

Another soldier—named only Walter—has been seen in one of the bedrooms. Wearing a beard and standing in a corner, Walter is not very fond of women, though he is harmless enough. Walter seems to have a great deal of anger—one assumes it stems from the violent and premature manner of his death.

Other spirits reside at Farnsworth House as well. One spirit named Mary is often felt and seems to project a protective presence in the house. She has been seen in corridors quite often, and others have seen her at the bottom of the stairs in the basement.

Farnsworth House was the first site in Gettysburg to offer ghost tours. When Patty first started sharing her uncanny experiences with the public in an impromptu theater setting, there were those who scoffed at such things. Soon, however, many people, hitherto reluctant to discuss their own encounters for fear of ridicule, came forward to tell Patty of their own otherworldly experiences at Gettysburg.

On one occasion, Vickie, a costumed interpreter, was sitting in the theater between tours, when suddenly her surroundings seemed strangely changed. She was still in the same basement, but it was not modern day— the basement appeared as it had in 1863! Appearing before Vickie were three Rebel soldiers, and they were carrying large boxes up the basement stairs. The men seemed quite solid and real. One of them, she recalled, wore a mustache. For an instant, Vickie had the very uncomfortable feeling that *she* was the ghost—not they!

At other times, visitors to the basement theater at Farnsworth have sworn they smelled gunpowder. Others have encountered cold spots, while still others have also seen the Rebel soldier with the mustache there.

A host of other paranormal phenomena, some related to the Civil War and others seemingly connected to previous residents of the house, have also been documented. Farnsworth House is one of the most haunted places in a town renowned for its abundance of ghosts in blue and gray.

In addition to comfortable lodgings, Farnsworth House offers ghost tours by costumed reenactors. For more information, write or call: Farnsworth House, 401 Baltimore Street, Gettysburg, PA 17325, (717) 334-8838.

16

BEHOLD A PALE RIDER: THE PHANTOM HORSEMAN OF LITTLE ROUND TOP

If, as historians suggest, the Battle of Gettysburg was the turning point of the war, then surely, the turning point of the battle itself was the desperate struggle for Little Round Top.

During this crucial encounter an unusual incident occurred. If true, the apparition seen by many on the field that day may well have changed the entire course of American history.

Throughout the first of July, Federal forces on the field had fought a holding action as they tried to contain determined Confederate assaults against the Union right flank. Pushed back onto Cemetery Ridge and its adjacent hills, the Union line held.

On July 2, it was the left flank's turn in hell. Heavy Rebel assaults pounded advanced Federal positions on the left, forcing them back toward the high ground. Late in the afternoon, one of the Union generals, to his horror, realized that there were no units at all defending the commanding heights of Little Round Top. The only Federal troops there was a small detachment of the Signal Corps, posted there to transmit messages to and from the front. A desperate race to beat the Rebels to the hill ensued, and several Federal regiments were hurriedly scraped together and thrown into line on the left.

Marching at double-quick time, the Union troops arrived on the slopes of Little Round Top only minutes ahead of the first wave of Longstreet's Confederates. Colonel Vincent, the brigade commander, pointed out in person the ground he wanted Colonel Chamberlain's Twentieth Maine to occupy.

The Twentieth Maine was posted to the extreme left of the Union line; Colonel Chamberlain's down-east regiment became the anchor on which the entire Federal line rested. If the Confederates could have turned that position, the whole Union line would have collapsed like a house of cards.

Chamberlain and his men were well aware of the importance of their position. Colonel Vincent's final words to him were, "Hold that ground at all hazards." It was the last time Chamberlain would see his brigade commander alive.

Chamberlain had little time to further contemplate the importance of his position. Even as the regiment took up a defensive line on the hill, they came under "constant and heavy" artillery fire. No sooner was the Twentieth Maine in line than a vigorous infantry assault on their right replaced the artillery barrage. The attack rapidly extended along the whole of the Twentieth's front. The action, Chamberlain reported, was "quite sharp and at close quarters."

Even as the regiment was heavily engaged, an officer from the center of the line informed Chamberlain that the enemy was maneuvering in the valley below, trying to work around behind the regiment's far left flank. Mounting a boulder to get a better look, Colonel Chamberlain could indeed see a larger body of Rebels moving behind the front, passing from the foot of Big Round Top over to his left.

Chamberlain immediately stretched his defensive line to the left, at the same time "refusing" his extreme left wing, so that it was bent at a sharp angle to the right. No sooner had the Twentieth Maine carried out this difficult maneuver, still under heavy fire, than the Confederates burst upon the newly extended left flank. They were repulsed only to charge again with even greater ferocity.

All along the line, for a full hour, the men of Longstreet's corps made desperate efforts to break the Union line and overrun the defenses at Little Round Top. Breakthroughs were made in many places, only to be repulsed after bitter, deadly hand-to-hand fighting.

The edge of the fight flowed backward and forward on the steep slope of the hill, like ocean waves crashing on the granite shores of Maine. Between attacks, the down-easterners gathered munitions from the cartridge boxes of the fallen, for by now their ammo was beginning to run short.

At this point, half of Chamberlain's left wing were already casualties, and a third of his whole command were either dead or wounded. What munitions were left had been robbed from the dead. It was at this critical juncture that a fresh enemy force appeared on the field.

As the Confederates closed on their position, it was clear they were in large numbers and were coming on," as if they meant to sweep everything before them." Chamberlain admitted that "it did not seem possible to withstand another shock like this now coming on."

The battle was at a crisis point. A roar of musketry to the rear of the Twentieth Maine also warned of a possible Rebel breakthrough behind them. The New Englanders' thin blue line was exhausted, out of ammo, and outnumbered. Defeat was imminent, and with it, the collapse of the whole Union line—perhaps of the very Union itself.

Miraculously, the inevitable did not happen. Something occurred that turned certain defeat into utter and complete victory. The truth of what occurred that afternoon on Little Round Top, however, is lost amidst the legend and the fog of war.

According to the official version, it was at this point that Colonel Chamberlain ordered his men to fix bayonets and charge. Amidst the deafening din of musketry—front and rear—and the blood-curdling Rebel yell, the Colonel reported "the word was enough." Supposedly the entire length of Chamberlain's overextended battle-line heard his order to fix bayonets and moved forward as one.

With a massive Rebel force but yards away, this thin blue line swept all before it. The fresh, well-armed Confederate force simply threw down their arms and surrendered! A second wave of Confederates also broke and ran without a shot being fired. Some four hundred prisoners, including two field officers and a large number of line officers, were captured from four different Rebel regiments—all by one bedraggled bunch of Yankees!

Something happened at Little Round Top alright— but not necessarily the way the official accounts would suggest. Soon after the battle, reports filtered out that during the crisis point of the battle, an apparition appeared, an apparition which had turned the tide of battle in favor of the Federal forces. The troops, it was said, beheld a pale rider in their midst. It had come from nowhere and was dressed in antique costume. It rode along the thin blue line of Federals, and everywhere it passed, men picked up hope and took courage in the fight.

The Rebels seemed to have seen the apparition as well. A number of them were seen to fire on it, thinking it a Union commander as it was also clad in blue. But despite their concentrated fire at the figure on horseback, bullets had no effect on it. Soon, the phantom rider, with its tricorner hat and turned-back coattails, had spread dismay and panic among the Rebel ranks.

Conversely, the men in blue were suddenly brimming with confidence, as if some great and charismatic leader had suddenly appeared in their midst to lead them to certain victory. Inspired by the apparition, the Twentieth Maine moved forward behind him, and despite their lack of numbers, their counter-attack proved irresistible.

It was only with difficulty that Chamberlain could restrain his men from pursuing the Rebels too far—some even boasting that they were "on the road to Richmond." In discussing the incident afterwards, soldiers reported that the phantom rider closely resembled portraits they had seen of George Washington. Well aware of the crucial role they had played in the battle, some ventured the theory that Washington had appeared to them in their hour of trial in order to save the very Union he had once fought so hard to establish.

On the face of it, the appearance of General Washington on the field of Gettysburg may seem outlandish. Yet, the War Department did not regard it so at the time. As rumors filtered back to Washington, D.C., Secretary of War Stanton dispatched a staff officer, Colonel Pittenger, to investigate. He interviewed a number of participants, including General Oliver O. Howard of Maine. He apparently gathered extensive eyewitness testimony of the incident; of course, his findings were never published. The official dispatches remained the accepted account of the battle, the one which historians have repeated without question ever since.

Beyond the issue of the official suppression of the facts, did the Ghost of George Washington really appear to the beleaguered troops at Little Round Top and lead them on to victory?

Of course, there are a number of alternatives for explaining the unofficial reports of the ghostly leader. One could dismiss it as merely a soldier's tale—a story told around the campfire to gullible recruits. Or, perhaps it was a mass hallucination, brought on by fatigue and the stress of battle. There is one other alternative even more outlandish than the original, yet one with some corroborating evidence to it. More than four score years before there had been another crisis point in American history; a moment when the fate of the nation hinged on the resolution of a few men in blue.

It was during the Revolutionary War that it happened. The winter of 1777 was a bad one, particularly for the troops at Valley Forge. The army nearly fell apart, save for the leadership of one man—George Washington. And by all accounts, an apparition appeared to him too.

Anthony Sherman had been with Washington at Valley Forge that terrible winter and was at headquarters one day when the general emerged from his quarters proclaiming he had had the strangest encounter. Washington was alone in his quarters when the room around him grew luminous. By all accounts Washington witnessed "dark manifestations"—black clouds, lightning, and the light of a thousand suns. The vision (if that is what it was) then began to become more specific. Washington witnessed the "thundering of the cannon, clashing of swords, and the shouts and cries of hundreds of thousands in mortal combat." Researchers who have studied this singular experience of Washington have interpreted at least part his vision as a remarkable premonition of the American Civil War—a few even say that it refers specifically to Gettysburg.

Here we have two unique events, both at a crisis point in American history, both involving Washington. In one, Federal troops claim to see Washington appear to them. In the other, Washington witnesses a body of troops clad in blue in a desperate battle. Could these two events have somehow occurred simultaneously in the time-space continuum?

Terms like astral projection and bilocation are bandied about quite a bit these days—perhaps too much so. Nevertheless, they are not new concepts, nor are they without any foundation in fact. In the Middle Ages it was reported that both saints and witches were able to appear in two places at the same time. In more recent times, there have been a number of documented accounts of people appearing—and disappearing—in broad daylight in widely separated parts of the globe. On rare occasions, for reasons still unknown, persons have been able to project some aspect of their essence across time and space.

It has been theorized that some apparitions are neither spirits of the dead nor the residual memory of a bygone event; rather, they are still living beings. Farfetched? Perhaps so; but if such a phenomenon defies the rules of logic, it does not necessarily defy the laws of physics. The common conception of time-space is akin to a train traveling on a set of railroad tracks across the prairie—running straight as an arrow in one direction to infinity. If one accepts Albert Einstein's pronouncements on the subject, however, time-space is more like the tracks of a roller-coaster in the amusement park, twisting, turning, and doubling back upon itself. So long as we stay contained within our own compartment, without reference to any other segment of the track, we seem to be going forward in a regular and predictable manner.

But maybe, just maybe, at certain times and certain places, and for reasons we cannot fathom, the blinders we wear that keep us from communication with the past or future are somehow removed, if only for a brief moment. Could such an event have happened on July 2, 1863?

Supernatural or super-science, the incident at Little Round Top remains a most strange occurrence, even for those well versed in the mysteries of the ghosts and haunts of the Civil War.

17

THE BLACK BOAR
OF DOOM

Many of the folk who settled the South were of Irish and Scots-Irish ancestry. Among the Celtic folk of western Britain, there was a long-held belief that the devil sometimes took the form of a black hog. Perhaps that in part explains the reports among certain Confederate regiments in the western theater of the war.

During the early days of the war, some Rebel troops of southeastern Missouri had the notion that their unit was haunted by a Black Boar of Doom. These tough cavalrymen claimed that every time one of their number saw the Black Boar just before a battle, it presaged his death in action. The boar was a monstrous-looking beast—big, black as night, and with eyes like two burning coals. An encounter with this spectral beast was indeed a terrifying event. No man who saw it, they said, ever lived more than seven days.

One cavalryman of the regiment was undaunted, however. He did not believe in ghosts and scoffed at the superstitions of his fellow troopers. Right before a major battle, the soldier saw the Black Boar. He was still undaunted; a hog is a hog, he said, no matter how unusual it seems. A skeptic by nature, nothing could persuade him it was anything other than an overgrown razorback.

Soon after he saw the beast, his unit was engaged in a big battle. Casualties were high. But this skeptic came through it all unscathed. He went about camp bragging that he'd seen the boar and survived, and goading his messmates for being so gullible.

The next evening, the trooper and his messmates were inspecting some of the booty they had liberated from the Yankees. One of their number was inspecting a newfangled Yankee revolver. It was one of the new, double-action guns with a self-cocking mechanism. Not familiar with its operation, the Johnny Reb inspecting it accidentally discharged the gun. The bullet made a beeline for the skeptic's skull, plowing through the trooper's brain and killing him instantly. The Black Boar had claimed yet another victim.

18

A Spectral Tour of Vicksburg

*Vicksburg contains many of my old pupils
and friends; should it fall into our hands, I will
treat them with kindness, but they have sowed
the wind and must reap the whirlwind.*
—William T. Sherman, June 27, 1863

The struggle for control of the strategic river port of Vicksburg, Mississippi, in the summer of 1863 is considered one of the greatest sieges of modern history. Gen. Ulysses S. Grant's dogged persistence in capturing the crucial stronghold was matched only by the determination of General Pemberton's Confederates to resist to the last extremity. Caught between the two contending forces were the civilians of Vicksburg.

Throughout the spring and summer of 1863, the city of Vicksburg endured the siege of Grant's army. Bombarded daily by large siege and naval cannon, soldier and civilian alike watched daily as food dwindled and disease became rampant. Though the actual number of civilian deaths due to gunfire was small, their suffering was still great, and many deaths were due indirectly to the siege, through starvation and disease. With such widespread pain and privation at Vicksburg, it is no surprise that it finds a reflection on the spectral plane.

McRaven House may justly lay claim to be the house with the most spectral disturbances related to the Civil War in Vicksburg. Begun in 1750, the house had already seen many changes by the time war came to Vicksburg. During the siege, the house was used as a field hospital, and several bullets found with teeth marks on them, testify to the suffering of the wounded there. Many of the spectral disturbances in the house are believed to originate from the soldiers who died there.

The best-known of McRaven's haunts are connected to the period right after the fall of the city, when Vicksburg was under Federal occupation. According to one story, right after the fall the house was used as headquarters by the Union commandant. One night a junior officer was murdered by some Rebel sympathizers and his body dumped in the Mississippi. A stickler for duty, the dead officer allegedly appeared before the colonel to report his own death!

A more likely candidate for the primary resident spook at McRaven House, however, is John Bobb, the man who lived there at the time. During the Yankee occupation in 1864, some Union soldiers were trespassing on his property, by all accounts drunk and disorderly. To encourage them to leave, Bobb threw a brick at them. The soldiers returned to their barracks to get their guns and dragged the old man from the property, took him to a secluded location, and filled him full of lead. They were never punished. Bobb threw brickbats at McRaven nevermore.

When the current owner of the property, Leland French, first took possession of the house some years back, he was busy restoring a room one day when the phone rang. Going over to pick up the phone, something—something big—hit him from behind so hard that his glasses shattered, and he required stitches for his face. Later, when Leland told one of the previous owners, Brad Bradway, of the incident, Bradway said cryptically, "Oh, that's just one of the bad boys that comes around once in a while."

At this point Leland invited an Episcopal priest to come and bless the house. After that exorcism all the spectral visitations have been of a benign nature, and no malevolent spirits currently reside in McRaven anymore. From time to time spirits clad in uniform have been sighted in the house, along with a woman dressed in brown. There is also an active spirit that is fond of playing with the lights.

One night, a group of Civil War reenactors were staying in the house and were serenaded to music on the piano by "Miss Annie"—which would not have been unusual, save for the fact that she had been dead for over one hundred years! Later that same night, they were surprised when one of the lamps came on all by itself. What was doubly odd about it was that the lamp was not even plugged in.

No one is quite certain how many ghosts still haunt McRaven; Walt Grayson, a television producer who has filmed a number of documentaries on Mississippi ghosts—including McRaven's—has described the house as "the most haunted house in Mississippi." It is believed that at least five former residents still haunt the place, not including many other stray specters.

Anchuca, a grand antebellum mansion on East First Street, was built in 1830. Its Greek Revival architecture speaks to the visitor of an elegant and more gracious era. At one time it was owned by Joseph Davis, brother of Confederate president Jefferson Davis, and Jeff Davis himself once addressed the citizens of the city from its second story balcony.

By all accounts, a female ghost inhabits the halls of Anchuca. She has been most often seen in the parlor, standing before the fireplace in a brown dress. Her features are those of a young woman, perhaps one of the many brave young ladies who endured famine and disease during the siege. Some say she was the daughter of an earlier owner who forbade her marriage to a man beneath her station, and that she died of a broken heart. Either way, this fetching female phantom seems perfectly at home in this antebellum bed and breakfast.

The Duff Green mansion, just down the block from Anchuca, also has a reputation for being haunted. During the siege it was used as a hospital for Confederate casualties, and by all accounts, those who died there may well have never left.

Former owners of Duff Green have reported hearing the sound of people walking across the second floor when no one is up there. Some say it is the sound of dead soldiers looking for their amputated limbs. Today, the house serves not as hospital, but as an elegant bed and breakfast featuring cozy evening cocktails and a relaxing pool for August evening swims. The ghosts come at no additional charge.

Not all Vicksburgers were dyed-in-the-cotton Confederates. The Klein family, owners of beautiful Cedar Grove, were staunch Unionists—and by some accounts paid a terrible price for it. Built in 1840, and still one of the largest antebellum homes in the South, before the war Cedar Grove's elegant halls hosted formal balls for the elite of Dixie, including Jefferson Davis and his willful wife, Varina. But John Klein's wife, Elizabeth, was an Ohio native and a close relative of William Tecumseh Sherman, the hated Yankee general who began the siege of the city. That fact, of course, did not make the house immune to artillery shells. Some of the first shots fired at the city went through the walls of Cedar Grove; one of them is still embedded in the parlor wall.

Soon after the bombardment of the city began, General Sherman himself escorted the Klein clan to safety and gave them assurances their home would be spared destruction. Union troops took over the house for the duration, and General Grant is thought to have slept in the massive four-poster bed that graces the master bedroom—now called the Grant Room.

While Cedar Grove and the Kleins survived the siege and the war, locals said the family was cursed, and doubly so; not only had they sided with the Yankees, but they even named their son Willie for the hated Yankee general, William T. Sherman. Folks say that was the real cause of the accidental shooting of sixteen-year-old Willie on the back stairs of the house. Moreover, the Kleins had ten children, yet only six survived into adulthood. This tragic history helps explain the sounds of children so often heard when no children are present. Employees say the sound of a baby crying resounds in the nursery, and sounds of children scurrying around the house are sometimes heard as well.

Visitors will occasionally see shadowy figures at Cedar Grove, but the most common spectral presences reported are sounds in the night. One former manager reported hearing a scream and the sound of someone falling down the back stairs; perhaps it was a spectral memory of the death of Willie Klein. At other times, workers have felt something invisible rush past them in the halls of Cedar Grove.

The patriarch of the Klein family, John Klein, also makes his presence known. Even though the inn has long since been a smoke-free facility, guests, owners and hostesses have all smelled a distinct aroma of tobacco in the old gentleman's parlor from time to time. It is known that John Klein would smoke his pipe in that room daily before retiring for the night. Old habits, apparently, die hard.

The people of Vicksburg have the reputation for being a stubborn lot. Having surrendered on the fourth of July to the Yankees, they refused to celebrate that holiday again until 1945. Likewise, the people of the city, despite war, reconstruction, and an annual modern Yankee invasion from the North, persist in retaining their traditional love of gracious living and hospitality.

Their ghosts, too, are a persistent lot. Perhaps that is why Vicksburg still is host to so many. It seems that given a choice between Vicksburg and heaven, quite a few have preferred Vicksburg.

19

THE WHITE LADY OF CHICKAMAUGA

The Indians called it the "River of Death." But today, Chickamauga, despite its ominous name, is a quiet little stream, one of many that feed the Tennessee River. During the War Between the States, however, the little stream justified its title many times over.

Chickamauga was one of the war's bloodiest clashes. For three days, two mighty armies contended for control of northern Georgia and Chattanooga. Finally, a tragic error by the Federals allowed a Confederate corps under Gen. James Longstreet to pierce the Union right wing, rolling up the Yankee flank and causing a wholesale collapse of the Federal line. Had not Gen. George Thomas, in charge of the left wing of the Union army, held firm, the Army of the Cumberland would have been annihilated right there. As it transpired, it was still a very near thing. In the end, nearly a third of all combatants were casualties, with thousands missing on both sides.

Perhaps because of this legacy of death, an ominous aura to this day hangs over the land through which the Chickamauga flows. Both locals and visitors report strange sights on the old fields of battle. It is not uncommon for locals to take a short cut through the park to get home, and they commonly report of one minute driving through sunlit countryside, the next minute to be plunged into a thick and enveloping fog on entering the battlefield.

A strange mist it is, that only dwells where the battle once raged, and many a native Georgian can tell you of strange things seen as they hurried home. Visitors, too, have had their encounters, as have the park personnel from time to time. Chickamauga is a large park, spanning a broad expanse of Georgia countryside, and a host of different ghosts and other strange things have been reported there over the years. One of the most persistent of these is the entity they call the White Lady of Chickamauga.

After the battle, the armies had moved on, leaving in their wake untold carnage. Caissons and cannon, broken and battered, amply littered the field. Dead draft animals and cavalry mounts were scattered about in abundance. But most common, and saddest of all, was the vast human wreckage the armies left behind.

Everywhere near the scene of battle, barns and homes were converted into makeshift hospitals for the thousands hurt in battle. Many local folk were searching amid the carnage for a lost relative or lover. For many who lived nearby, Bragg's Confederates were not some impersonal army that came from afar, but a gray host of friends, relatives, and neighbors.

Picking their way among the broken barricades, stepping over mangled corpses that lay thick upon the field, many such civilians could not rest till they had found those whom they loved best. Some were found among the wounded—injured but alive. Others were, at length, discovered in remote corners of the battlefield, lying where they had fallen, and were removed to a family graveyard. But there were others—too many others—whose bodies were never found.

Of the Confederate forces engaged in the battle, some fifteen hundred remained missing after the battle. The Federals had some five thousand missing. All were presumed dead. Strange thing is, their bodies were never recovered. Still their wives and mothers and lovers roamed the battlefield searching out their mortal remains.

One such lady was Abigail Reed. She had been engaged to a young Confederate from the area, John Ingraham. Johnny had marched off to war, bedecked in her homespun gray, with high hopes of coming back to make Abigail his bride. But Johnny never came marching home again; Abigail Reed found him on the battlefield and buried him close to where he lay. To this day Reed Bridge—in the park—bears her name to commemorate her loss.

Another young woman, much like sad Abigail, searched the fields in vain. Wherever she went, she asked soldiers about her missing beau. But all whom she met, when she gave his name and described his face, sadly shook their heads and said they hadn't seen anyone like that, living or dead.

It is certain that she was a new bride or a bride-to-be, for those who saw her agree she was clad all in white. Long after other friends and relatives gave up their searches, the White Lady of Chickamauga continued her mournful quest. Over the rocks and into the glens, through the thick forest, she searched for some hint, some trace of her lost love. At night she held her lantern aloft, and the flickering light became a familiar sight on the empty fields of Chickamauga Creek.

To her dying day, the local folk still say, the White Lady of Chickamauga never gave up her quest. She was buried in the white bridal gown she so longed to wear for her lover. When they laid the clods of dirt over her coffin, everyone thought that was the end of it, and a sad ending at that. But even after she was laid in the ground, people still saw a bobbing, flitting light on the battlefield, around the places they had previously seen her search in vain.

That was how, one supposes, the legend of the White Lady of Chickamauga got started among the locals. Strange thing is, though, that visitors to the park who have never heard the tale have also had encounters with the White Lady. She is most often seen near the time of the original battle, in September and October, bedecked in an elaborate white period gown. She looks normal except for a slight luminous glow, but she seems intractably absorbed in her search.

At other times, people have simply seen an odd light—a ghost light they call it—roaming the park as if it had some purpose behind it. Whether this light is one and the same with the White Lady or something else is unknown. Both remain a mystery—one of many that still dwell by the waters of the "River of Death."

20

THE JINGLING HOLE

One of the enduring myths of the Civil War is that the conflict was simply a conflict between North and South. The true conflict, however, was a more complex affair. Many people up north were sympathetic to the Confederate cause, and others were extremely hostile to the notion of abolition. Conversely, there were those south of the Mason-Dixon Line who remained loyal to the Union. In many areas, this conflict of loyalties broke out into open warfare—a civil war within the Civil War.

East Tennessee and the western reaches of North Carolina made up one such area. This area had never been a big slave-owning region, and when the Confederate government began drafting all free white males—except those owning twenty or more slaves—many of the fiercely independent mountaineers resented it deeply. Mountain folk had always been quick to resort to the gun to settle disputes, and it was not long before bands of Unionist guerrillas were roaming the mountains, harassing Confederate garrisons and ambushing patrols. Secessionist sympathizers soon responded in kind. It was a nasty and deadly little affair, with neighbor murdering neighbor and no quarter given. One legacy of this bitter harvest of hate was the Jingling Hole.

A section of the Appalachians where the Carolina border butts up against Tennessee was where the fighting was particularly intense. So much so, in fact, it earned the nickname the "Bloody Third." If a guerrilla was so unlucky as to be taken alive by his foes, they would often not kill him outright. Rather, they would have a little sport with him first. He would be taken to a place called the Jingling Hole.

The Hole was a deep, deep pit with water at the bottom. Whether it had been a natural shaft originally is not recorded, but it had been "improved" to make it more useful to the bushwhackers and guerrillas of both sides. They placed an iron bar over the opening, strong enough to support the weight of a man. The bar was also just the right thickness for a man to wrap his hands around.

A prisoner would be taken to the Jingling Hole and at gunpoint be made to grip the iron bar and hang from it suspended over the pit. At first they just let the prisoner dangle there a while, laughing and making crude jokes as his hands gradually went numb. Then he would finally lose his grip and plunge into the blackness of the pit. After a time, though, this sport got a little dull, so they improved on it a bit.

As a prisoner dangled over the abyss, the booted bushwhackers would proceed to stamp on his hands. First one hand, then the other, then back to the first. As they pounded their victim's hands with their boot heels, their spurs would jingle a sprightly rhythm punctuated by the occasional cry of pain from the poor prisoner. Hence, the name Jingling Hole.

If a man had enough grit and endurance, he might survive long enough for the bushwhackers to tire of the game. If they felt generous, they might even let the prisoner go. More often, though, the victim would lose out to the pain and the strain on his muscles, and plunge into the dark abyss. Sometimes, it would be all over quickly. More likely, the water at the bottom would cushion his fall just enough that, though injured, he would still be alive. The victim would pad about in the dank dark, crying in vain for help, until at last he gave up the ghost and drowned. In either case, it was a bad way to go.

The Jingling Hole is still on that mountainside in the Smokies. The local folk don't talk about it much anymore, and the young folk have all but forgotten about it. But it is still an ill-omened place avoided by all but the foolhardy.

They say that if you go up there by the dark of the moon, you may still hear weird sounds. There are the moans and groans that echo from the deep hole, sounding for all the world like the cries of the damned in Hell. They echo from deep within the bowels of the earth. Then too, you might hear a high-pitched tinkling sound; the sound, they say, of the ringing and jingling of the bushwhackers' spurs resounds off the rocks as their owners have their sport. It is at these times indeed, that this dark and sinister place continues to earn its nickname—the Jingling Hole.

21

QUANTRILL'S
HAUNTED HOARD

O f all the Union and Confederate guerrilla bands, surely the most famous—or infamous—was that of William Clarke Quantrill. Depending on who you listen to, they were either bold and brave freedom fighters or vicious terrorists—perhaps a little of both.

By Quantrill's own account, he never had any intention of becoming a Confederate guerrilla. Originally from Ohio, he taught school in both Kansas and Missouri for a while before the war. Then one day, he and his brother got the notion in their heads to head west for Colorado.

They had not gotten out of Kansas when they were attacked by a band of thirty Kansas Red Legs. William's brother was killed immediately, and they riddled William so full of lead they thought him dead as well. Supposedly, the Red Legs were a vigilante group of free-staters, high-minded citizens opposed to the extension of slavery in the western territories. Land pirates was more like it. The Quantrill brothers had been attacked solely with intent to murder, pillage, and plunder.

For three days, Quantrill lay there, more dead than alive. An old Indian looking for his lost dog, found Quantrill and nursed him back to health in his camp. He stayed with the Indian for four months. As he regained his strength, his benefactor tracked his stolen wagon and team to Lawrence, Kansas. After several days of quiet investigation, the Indian scout learned the names of all thirty men who had assaulted Quantrill and murdered his brother—respectable citizens all.

The names of those thirty were seared into Quantrill's heart like a branding iron. He vowed then and there that one day he would avenge himself against them all. Whatever motive other men may have had for fighting under the black banner, Quantrill's war had little to do with slavery or secession. Border ruffians and bushwhackers had been active along the Kansas-Missouri border since well before the Civil War, and the outbreak of formal hostilities in 1861 only served to make the vicious little war there even more vicious.

Things came to a head in 1863 when the Union commandant of the border district, Gen. Thomas Ewing, began arresting women suspected of aiding the Confederate guerrillas. The term *concentration camp* was unknown then, but that was precisely what General Ewing intended to create when he began rounding up noncombatants and crowding them into a rickety old building in Kansas City. When the building collapsed on August 14, killing four women and maiming scores more, Missourians were appalled.

General Ewing's intolerable act was followed a short time later by an even more intolerable act: General Order 11. Order 11 dictated that all civilians in the western border counties of Missouri were to be rounded up and driven into exile. Any man, woman, or child found still in their homes would be shot on sight. With such actions on the part of the Federals, it was inevitable the Rebels would retaliate.

They say that revenge is a dish best eaten cold. The time was ripe for Quantrill to even up old scores in

Lawrence, Kansas—and now there were others with personal grudges to settle there as well. Whatever crimes the Rebel guerrillas may have committed in their campaigns against the pro-Union forces, making war on women and children was not one of them.

Their numbers swollen to nearly five hundred men because of Yankee outrages against their kinfolk, a vengeful guerrilla army descended on Lawrence, Kansas on August 21, 1863. Thundering into town at daybreak, for three hours the guerrillas vented the full fury of their rage on the town of Lawrence. There are many things one may say about the raid on Lawrence, but random or senseless it was not. There was a cold-blooded logic behind the killing by Quantrill's men.

Before the raid, Quantrill and his captains drew up a list of men to be killed. These men were dragged from their homes and summarily executed. In another time and place, such guerillas may have labeled their victims counterrevolutionaries and held a mock trial before they killed them. But though the guerrillas were many things, they were not hypocrites. It was an eye for an eye, pure and simple.

Only one man on the hit list escaped—the one at the very top: Senator Jim Lane, leader of the Red Legs. A man with a guilty conscience often develops quick reflexes. When Lane heard the sound of horsemen approaching town, he high-tailed it, still in his night-shirt, to a nearby cornfield and hid there till the killing and burning were over. When the guerrillas departed Lawrence, they left behind a town in flames, with four score newly made widows, and 150 fresh Red Leg corpses. To the guerrillas' credit, no woman was harmed in any way during the raid, violent as it was.

Besides accomplishing their bloody mission, Quantrill and his men helped themselves to as much plunder as they could cart away. Horses laden down with bags of gold and silver, however, do not make for great haste, and after Lawrence, things became rather hot for the guerrillas. Quantrill and a few trusted lieutenants secretly buried their hoard of loot in a convenient place near Independence, Missouri. It seems likely, too, that several of the guerrillas who died from their wounds may have been buried with the treasure. Quantrill and his men had every intention of going back and retrieving their booty when the Yankees were no longer hot on their trail, but things did not turn out that way.

One by one, Quantrill's followers left or were killed off by the Yankees. Quantrill realized that their cause was hopeless; sooner or later, Lee and the other Rebel generals would have to surrender. But he also realized that for him, there could be no surrendering. Eventually, Quantrill himself fell, riddled with bullets, in the neighboring state of Kentucky.

After the war, a number of folk tried to find Quantrill's buried treasure, to no avail. Although the general neighborhood of where it was hidden was known, knowledge of its exact location had died with Quantrill. Nevertheless, there was an even more serious difficulty connected with recovering the treasure: the hoard was cursed.

There was little question that Quantrill's hoard was blood money. It had been obtained over the bodies of 150 Kansans, and there was just no cleansing away the taint on that money. That, however, did not stop anybody from trying to find it. There were, of course, some relatives of the dead guerrillas, who may have had a good idea of where the treasure lay. By all accounts, though, anyone approaching the secret cache was confronted by an array of supernatural barriers. For one thing, ghosts dressed in butternut brown uniforms were reported to confront anyone who approached. In addition, bluish-colored ghost lights dancing among the bushes would appear as treasure hunters came near. Should anyone still not be deterred, the minute they touched spade to ground and tried to dig up the gold, they received a jolt, like they had been struck by lightning.

Rumor had it in Independence that women were immune to these spectral shenanigans. Around the turn of the century, at least one female treasure seeker tried to obtain Quantrill's treasure. As the woman struck her shovel into the earth, however, a shower of dazzling sparks burst from the soil. The woman was hurled backwards by the jolt of energy and knocked unconscious.

Her two male cohorts, who had stood a safe distance away, ran forward, grabbed her under the arms, and dragged her back to the wagon. As the party retreated, hundreds of lights leapt into the air as if exulting in victory over those who would take from the owners their ill-gotten gains.

PART FOUR
REAPING THE WHIRLWIND

As the war progressed into its final stages, the conflict took a distinctly malicious turn. The Union Army, to hasten the end, employed "scorched earth" tactics more and more often. Such ruthless campaigns must inevitably have long-term effects. And as the end neared, and the fighting became bloodier, it became even more apparent that the cause was lost. Yet, still the men in gray kept fighting, even when they knew that death and defeat were inevitable. Many of these men still seem to be carrying on the struggle—only on the spirit plane.

22

GRAY GHOSTS OF MOSBY'S RANGERS

Col. John Singleton Mosby was commander of the 43rd Battalion, Virginia Cavalry, CSA—Mosby's rangers. More than a century and a quarter later, Mosby remains the partisan leader par excellence. They called Mosby the Gray Ghost of the Confederacy. His elusiveness and audacious tactics gave him and his rangers an almost supernatural aura. He was able to appear at will behind enemy lines, attack Union supply lines, raid garrisons, and wreak havoc with enemy railroads. Yet, Mosby and his men were always able to blend into the countryside afterwards.

Colonel Mosby, unlike other partisan leaders, survived the war, and lived to a ripe old age. Though nicknamed the Gray Ghost, no report has ever surfaced of him haunting his old stomping grounds. The same may not be said, however, of some of his soldiers. During the fall of 1864, one incident in particular occurred which seems to have had a profound spectral consequence that may still be plaguing the region. In August, Gen. Phil Sheridan was sent into the Shenandoah to rid it of all Southern forces and to put an end to the Valley's usefulness to the Confederacy. Throughout the war, Lee had used the Shenandoah as both granary with which to feed his troops and as an invasion route to attack Federal forces with impunity.

Though the massive Federal army seemed to have little trouble dealing with the regular Confederate units in the Valley, dealing with Mosby's rangers proved a more difficult task. Six days after Sheridan's army arrived in the valley, Mosby's men captured and burned the Union cavalry's supply train on the road near Berryville, Virginia—virtually under the eyes of their commanders. Outraged at Mosby's impertinence, Sheridan ordered a "scorched earth" campaign against the surrounding region.

As Mosby's men were largely drawn from the local populace, the burning of the Valley farms could not help but be taken personally. Though Grant had given Sheridan orders to have Mosby's men summarily executed if captured, Sheridan refrained from violating the rules of war, knowing that it could lead to reprisals against his men. Nonetheless, the duel between the two sides quickly devolved into a grudge match.

On September 23, while Mosby was out of action with a gunshot wound, a detachment of his rangers had a skirmish with Yankee cavalry. Rangers attacked the rear of a Federal column, thinking it was a small detachment. It turned out to be the rearguard of two divisions of Sheridan's Cavalry Corps.

Quickly, the roles of the fox and the hound were reversed, with a horde of Yankee cavalry in hot pursuit of the rangers. A running fight developed over fields and along country roads in the area south and east of Front Royal, the county seat of Warren County.

None of Mosby's men died in the fight, but a Union officer, Lieutenant McMaster, was killed after being unhorsed. The Federals claimed that he had been murdered after surrendering. The Rebels vehemently denied the charge, saying that McMaster had continued to fight dismounted.

Regardless, the Federals, having taken six rangers prisoner, dragged them into Front Royal where they strung up two of them and shot down the other four in cold blood. When Mosby returned to duty and learned of the outrage, the partisan leader felt obliged to retaliate. When the rangers had accumulated thirty captives, Mosby had the prisoners draw lots choosing seven of them for reprisal.

Reluctantly, in the same manner that their own men had been killed by the Yankees, the rangers hanged and shot the seven Union soldiers. Albeit, only three of the Federals were actually killed. Still, the point had been made, and the Yankees did not abuse any more of Mosby's men.

Front Royal, the town where Sheridan's troops murdered the rangers, was called Helltown in frontier days. The Federals apparently had sought to make Front Royal live up to its original name. There is some evidence to suggest they succeeded, at least in part. Beginning in 1870, and continuing in approximately six-year intervals well into the twentieth century, the community of Front Royal has been visited by a most appalling apparition.

A local squire who encountered this entity called it the Whirlaway. Characterized by a violent outburst of wind shrieking through field and forest, the apparition at first appears to folk as a silver-green light that shimmers before the eye.

Out of this bright display of light emerges a figure, wearing a plain gray jacket and trousers, with a visored kepi shading its face. Surrounded by a shining silver glow, to mortal eyes it seems as though one is looking at him underwater. The strange apparition is able to move faster than the eye can follow. Even standing still it appears to undulate.

The best documented appearance of the Whirlaway was in 1925. In the early autumn of that year, Mrs. Cook, a local resident, and her daughters were virtually besieged by the Whirlaway. Their house lay on a stone outcropping overlooking the Shenandoah, in the Riverton community near to Front Royal. That day the Cooks first felt a strong wind coming out of the river, then they heard the sound of heavy boots on the gravel path leading up to their house. As it coalesced into human form, the four women quickly bolted and barred every window and door. Yet the entity seemed able to move from the front to the back of the house in the blink of an eye. Fortunately, the entity never got in the house, though the women were terrorized by it for the better part of the afternoon. That same day, the Whirlaway paid a visit to folks on the other side of the river as well. Some years before that incident, Judge Sanford Johnson of Front Royal also had a terrifying encounter with the entity.

Who, or what, was the Whirlaway? According to local tradition, it may be a young man of the Civil War era who had inquired about joining Mosby's command. Mistaken for a guerrilla, the Yankees fell upon the lad with murderous intent. When they had finished with him, they dumped his body in front of a herd of stampeding cattle.

Whether the young man actually rode with Mosby or not is a moot point; local tradition claims he was a civilian. Yet, Mosby's men had only the simplest of uniforms—generally something gray—and they were recruited from, fought around, and lived among the local populace. Their ability to merge into the civilian population was legendary, and so it may be true that the Whirlaway was actually one of Mosby's men.

In nearby Loudoun County, on a certain county road, local hunters have on occasion encountered phantom cavalry, riding hell-bent-for-leather down the road. No one is visible, but the rush of the wind as they ride past and the sounds of spurs jingling and sabers banging against their scabbards can be distinctly heard. Whether they are the ghosts of Mosby's men or his Yankee pursuers is not certain. What is for certain, however, is that the spirits of Mosby's rangers still dwell in the Shenandoah Valley.

23

THE RESTLESS SPIRITS
OF CEDAR CREEK

In the fall of 1864, Gen. Phil Sheridan, also known as "Little Phil," was ordered to scour the Shenandoah Valley. His instructions were clear: to sweep the valley of Confederate troops and destroy anything that could be of value to the war effort. Today, they would call it total war. In the autumn of 1864, the inhabitants of the Shenandoah simply referred to it as the Burning.

The southern high command realized the situation in the Shenandoah was critical. Yet the Confederates had only limited resources and manpower to deal with the threat—and Sheridan's army vastly outnumbered them. With only fifteen thousand men, it seemed General Jubal Early could do little more than annoy the pillaging Yankees.

By October 10, Sheridan's army was encamped beside the waters of Cedar Creek near the town of Middleton, Virginia. So confident was Sheridan of his military superiority, that he left his army to its own devices as he traveled to Washington to curry favor with his superiors. When he returned, he was in no hurry to rejoin his men in the field. Instead, he enjoyed the comforts of the Logan house in Winchester, some twenty miles away from camp.

While the Federals rested from their "scorched earth" campaign, a regimental band found time to hold concerts in the nearby Episcopal church. With all the firepower at their disposal, the Yankee troops had little to fear from any ragtag Rebel army—or so they thought.

Dawn of October 19 found the camps along Cedar Creek shrouded in fog. The sun rose, an angry crimson orb in the thick gray mist. As the Union troops moped about camp wiping the sleep from their eyes, the mist began to darken and take shape. Soon the gray fog coalesced into separate forms, coming closer to camp by the minute. Still the sleepy Federals noticed nothing odd. Only when the fog erupted in a thousand points of fire did the Yankees get their wakeup call. Taps—not reveille—would be played today.

Confederate scouts had discovered that the Federals at Cedar Creek had failed to set up proper pickets to guard the bivouac. When Early learned of this, he resolved to exploit his enemy's negligence and launch a surprise attack. Sending several divisions to work around the Yankee flank during the night, General Early placed his remaining troops under his own command for a frontal assault. This one-two punch, coupled with the element of surprise, proved devastating. In short order, three Union corps were overrun.

Like a house of cards, the Union army collapsed with only minimal resistance. Surprise turned to panic and panic into flight, as men ran for their lives, abandoning guns, equipment, and clothing to escape the vengeful Rebels. It would have been an overwhelming victory, save for two singular events.

Having routed a superior enemy force, the Confederates halted their pursuit to loot the Yankee camp. The famished and barefoot Rebel troops simply could not resist the temptation to help themselves to hot cooked food and new Yankee shoes. General Early, perhaps, thought the Yankees were so badly beaten that the leaderless mob retreating towards Middleton could be dealt with at leisure. He was wrong.

Jubal Early underestimated the feisty Phil Sheridan. When Sheridan heard the distant sound of gunfire, he knew at once that something was amiss. Hopping on his horse, Rienzi, the scrappy Union commander made a mad dash for Cedar Creek—a ride that would become legendary.

Sheridan ran smack into his retreating mob of soldiers—they could no longer be described as an army. Against all odds, however, through sheer will and charisma, "Little Phil" halted the rout. Soon he replaced panic and fear with discipline and resolve. Restoring order, he re-formed Union troops into a solid phalanx to meet the Rebels, who by now had resumed their pursuit. By late afternoon, Sheridan's men had counter-attacked. Now, it was the Southerners' turn to retreat. By the end of the day, Jubal Early's army had been decimated, and the bivouac at Cedar Creek was back in Union hands.

The church nearby was turned into a Union field hospital. Packed with maimed and mortally wounded men, the dead were hastily buried in the churchyard. The armies were soon gone and the battlefield cleared of debris. But there was one thing the burial and clean-up crews could not cleanse from Cedar Creek—the spirits of the restless dead.

The Union dead had been buried temporarily in the churchyard. It was not long, however, before workmen came to dig them up again and place them in plain pine boxes, preliminary to being shipped north. According to some the of the local folk, it was the digging up of the battle dead that set off the haunting of Cedar Creek.

The pine boxes had been piled up against the church like so much freight awaiting shipment. Residents began to see and hear strange things in the church late at night. A light would emerge from the church and go over to the wooden crates. It was as if someone or something was searching among the boxes with a candle. One night, a being more or less resembling a calf came out of the church. The beast walked around the grounds for a bit, then disappeared into thin air.

The pine coffins were finally sent north, but that did not put a stop to the spectral happenings along Cedar Creek. The ghosts were there to stay. People thereabouts could hear them, walking about, groaning, and carrying on late at night.

"Don't you hear the band?" folks would remark to one another. For on certain nights the sound of music could be heard eerily emanating from the little church. It was the same music that the regimental band had once practiced within its walls.

First a horn would start up; then a drum would begin to tap a beat; then the kettle drum would pitch in; and so on, until the whole ghostly ensemble would be performing its uncanny concert. To this day, they say, one can still hear odd knocking sounds within the old church.

Beginning not long after the war, elsewhere on the battlefield, farmers in the area would often hear the sounds of guns being discharged, while along the back lanes of the area, the clip-clop of phantom horses would resound, coming right up to a person without being caught sight of by anyone.

One farmer, however, did discover some quite visible ghosts. He was returning from a prayer meeting one evening around 10 P.M. Riding along, he thought he heard a bugle's sound and a drum beating. Halting his horse to listen better, the farmer saw a phantom officer walking ahead of a ghostly detachment of soldiers. The phantom officer called "Halt!" and the phantom column came to an abrupt stop. The spirits paid no heed to the passing farmer, and soon, when the bugle sounded again, the phantom host moved on.

Down close to the creek there stood an old barn, which had been in the middle of the battle. Some years back, a farmer named Holt Hottel had been leasing the property. One evening at dusk, he went into the barn to feed the horses and was throwing some hay down for them from the loft, when he noticed someone in the barn.

Thinking it was a vagrant, Holt yelled, "git out of hyar. I don't allow no tramps in the barn." The stranger just stood there and did not say anything. Holt got mad when the man refused to move on and lunged at him with the pitchfork, but the tines of the fork passed right through the dark figure. In terror, Holt jumped out of the loft and ran for dear life. Needless to say, the horses did not get fed that night.

At first, Holt's family and friends did not believe him when he told of the ghost. But soon, as others also began to encounter the same spirit, people stopped laughing, and started visiting the barn to see for themselves.

The ghost had on Yankee clothes and wore tall cavalry boots that came up to the thighs. He would only appear around dusk just after the sun had set. He would come out of the hayloft, halfway down the steps, and just stand there. The apparition was such a regular visitor that they began to bring railroad excursions out to the barn for people to see it.

Nearby, gracious Belle Grove Plantation was not immune to spectral visitors, either. In the plantation home of Belle Grove, one would often hear a carriage pull up in the middle of the night. A bell would ring, as if summoning the grooms to come out and handle the team. Yet, when the members of the household would come out, no one would ever be there.

Inside the mansion itself, they had one room with a door that would not stay shut. The residents repeatedly tried to close it, yet no sooner would one sit down, than the door would swing open again.

After the Battle of Cedar Creek, Sheridan had used Belle Grove as his field headquarters. It is believed that some of the many strange phenomena observed there are also associated with the battle and its aftermath.

For one thing, Belle Grove was the place to which Confederate general Stephen Ramseur, mortally wounded, was taken after the battle. Ramseur had commanded Early's advance guard during the initial attack on the Union camp. Ramseur had been in the forefront of battle throughout the day, and when Sheridan counterattacked, it was Ramseur's division that resisted the longest, lasting until Ramseur himself was cut down. Retreating back through the town of Strasburg, the wounded general was captured and taken to Belle Grove.

Although in the hands of the enemy, when he arrived at Sheridan's headquarters, the Confederate found, ironically, that he was among old friends. As he lay dying in the front parlor, gathered around Ramseur were old classmates from West Point and former comrades from the old days—George Armstrong Custer, Wesley Merritt, Colonel Henry DuPont, and others, now all Union commanders. Ramseur was still conscious when brought in, and the men had a bittersweet reunion before he died.

Since that day, on at least one known occasion, visitors to modern Belle Grove have seen a similar assemblage of blue and gray in that same room. Visitors have assumed it to be a group of Civil War buffs dressed in costume. But upon inquiring to the staff, they find to their surprise that such is not the case—no costumed male interpreters had been on the grounds.

A short time before the battle, another tragedy had been played out on the grounds of Belle Grove. Benjamin Coolie, the owner of the estate, had taken a beautiful wife, to whom the cook had developed a grudge. One day, Mrs. Coolie went to see how supper was progressing, whereupon the cook proceeded to take an axe to the mistress's head. The cook dragged the body out the door and along the flagstone walk, trailing blood and gore as she went, then tossed the body in the smokehouse.

A passerby, however, had noticed the cook dragging the body, and she was arrested and convicted of the crime. She would have been executed as well, had not the Yankees captured the county seat and let all the prisoners free from the county jail.

Since that time, Mrs. Coolie has been seen on numerous occasions at Belle Grove. Just last year, the curator had sent one of the house's antique rugs out to be specially cleaned by a firm in Front Royal. The museum staffer specifically instructed the dry cleaner not to deliver the rug during the weekend, as no would be there to receive it.

Come Monday morning, the staff arrived at Belle Grove and opened it up for the day, only to find the rug back in place inside the house! The delivery men for the cleaners, it seems, had ignored the curator's instructions and come by to deliver it on Saturday. By rights, they should have found the house locked up tight.

Instead, however, they found a woman, dressed in black, on the front porch. She did not speak, but simply pointed inside, to the room where the rug belonged. Not thinking twice, the men brought it in, laid it out, and left.

Many Southern mansions can boast of resident ghosts as part of their heritage, but only Belle Grove can claim one which accepts deliveries!

They say the Civil War has cast long shadows in the South; certainly there are no shadows longer than those in the Shenandoah. Just ask Mrs. Coolie.

24

ANDERSONVILLE APPARITIONS AND OTHER PHANTOM PRISONERS

The very name of Andersonville conjures up horrific visions of gaunt, emaciated prisoners looking like living skeletons, and of inhuman living conditions and physical abuse—scenes that have become all too familiar in the twentieth century. Other hellholes there most certainly were, but Andersonville remains the original symbol of the inhumanity of war.

Andersonville Prison became the most notorious of southern prisons during the war, but conditions there were far from unique. Other prisoners, both northern and southern, suffered conditions as bad as, and many times worse than Andersonville.

Ironically, Andersonville was intended as a way to improve the conditions for the South's prisoners of war. Elsewhere, prisoners had been confined to old dungeons and converted warehouses, deprived of light and fresh air. It was thought that by locating a new camp at Andersonville, Georgia, out in the countryside with an abundance of fresh air, light, and pure water, it would be better and more healthful. It would also serve to relieve overcrowding in other prisons.

In the end, things went horribly wrong. Due to war shortages, wooden barracks were never built. Then, because the North refused to continue exchanging prisoners, a camp designed to hold four thousand men was crowded with upwards of twenty thousand. It was a recipe for disaster.

Given this massive scale of suffering at Andersonville, one would assume there would be an over-abundance of spectral phenomena. While there have been several such reports emanating from the site of the camp, they do not seem to be nearly as numerous as one would expect. What has been seen there, however, has been most unusual.

In December of 1971, for example, three people were returning home one night from a civic club meeting in Americus, Georgia. As they passed by the road marker for Andersonville late at night, they saw a figure standing by the road. They had passed too quickly, though, to get a close look. He looked real enough, but was dressed in a most curious manner. He was dressed in military-style clothing, however, being midnight, they could not be certain of the color of the clothing. He wore a greatcoat and had what looked like a kepi on his head.

No sooner had they passed by him, than they turned the car around to get a closer look, so unusual did the man seem to them. But when they came back to the same spot, he was nowhere to be seen. It had not been more than a minute or two, and there was no place for anyone to hide near the road. Yet, the man had vanished into thin air.

In discussing the incident later, the trio all agreed that they had seen something out of the ordinary, perhaps supernatural. As they compared notes and discussed it with friends, they were convinced that the man's uniform was "old and odd"—more appropriate to the Civil War than anything of more recent vintage.

Speculation abounded locally as to who the apparition could be. Some suggested that it was the ghost of a dead Yankee prisoner. But that somehow did not fit what they had witnessed. The man did not look ragged nor emaciated, as a prisoner would be. Rather, he was very neatly dressed and well groomed, as befitted an officer, but there were no Union officers held at Andersonville.

In considering those connected with Andersonville who may have had some reason to haunt the place, far and away, the Confederate commandant Major Henry Wirz is the most likely candidate. Blamed for wartime conditions in the camp, he was put on trial as a war-criminal, convicted and hanged.

Modern opinion is unanimous in regarding Major Wirz as a victim of circumstance. Put in command of the camp late in the war, he had no responsibility for conditions inside the camp and tried to do what he could to correct them. His trial by the radical Republican administration after the war was a travesty. To his dying day, Wirz protested his conviction. As much as any of the dead at Andersonville, Wirz's restless spirit cries out for vindication.

More recently, a visitor to the national historic site at Andersonville encountered another of the camp's apparitions. This one was dressed neither in blue nor gray, but in black. Even more strange, the man carried an umbrella. When the visitor reported what he had seen to a park interpreter, the man did not seem surprised. Officially, of course, there are no ghosts at Andersonville, but the staff have become familiar with sightings of Father Whelan making the rounds. In June 1864 this Catholic chaplain came to the camp to minister to the prisoners, giving comfort—and last rites— where he was able. To judge by eyewitness accounts, the goodly pastor is still making his rounds.

While Andersonville was certainly the most notorious of prisons during the war, there were others with far higher death rates, and at the sites of other POW camps, the spirits of those who died are still quite evident.

At the site of Camp Hoffman in Maryland, sightings of phantom prisoners have not been limited to just visitors. Even park personnel have had experiences they cannot otherwise account for. But it is not northern soldiers whose restless wraiths wander the grounds, but those of Confederate prisoners.

Camp Hoffman was established in 1863 on a spit of land where the Potomac meets Chesapeake Bay—a place called Point Pleasant. Crammed with twice as many prisoners as it was designed to contain, thousands of prisoners died of typhus, dysentery, smallpox, and neglect.

Since its restoration and reopening as a state park in 1964, visitors, volunteers, and staff have all had spectral encounters. One park ranger, patrolling the park along Tour Route 5, spotted a uniformed man running across the road in his rearview mirror. When he craned his neck to see who it was, the man had vanished.

The state park also provides campgrounds where visitors can stay overnight. As a standard security practice, rangers patrol campgrounds where visitors stay overnight. A hospital and quarantine area for prisoners with smallpox was once located near the campground.

Late one night, Ranger April Havens was making her rounds on foot. Around 2 A.M., she was walking through Hoffman Circle toward the next campground when suddenly a queer feeling came over her. Instinctively, she turned around to see who or what might be behind her.

In the middle of the road she saw rows of white tents, arranged in military style. She turned back, then turned around again; they were still there. An indescribably eerie feeling overtook Havens as the realization of what she was witnessing sunk in.

The ranger, chilled and sweating at the same time, ran all the way back to the camp office. The ranger had no doubt about what she had witnessed.

In another instance, two campers were walking along the path on the Greene Loop camping area when they were joined by a third hiker. This man, however, was clad in Civil War costume and carried an old percussion musket. At first glance, they thought him to be just another reenactor visiting the park. The three walked along some thirty feet together, when suddenly, the soldier vanished into the air.

Elsewhere at Point Lookout Park, other psychic incidents have been well documented, such as a dog barking at people walking past who are not visible to the human eye; people being touched by invisible hands, and periodic sightings of soldiers in blue and gray throughout the park.

A psychic investigation team, including the famous ghost-hunter Hans Holzer, documented voices from another era on tape—all of them gathered from places in the park associated with the Civil War. Even in Boston Harbor, at old Fort Warren, ghosts of Confederate prisoners of war have been sighted.

Spectral memories seem to be common where such suffering in confined quarters has taken place. Whether ghosts in gray, or wraiths in blue, the lingering remnants of their emotional trauma lingers in the air at such places. "The evil that men do lives after them" it has been said. So it would seem with the horrors of Andersonville and other places where phantom prisoners of the Civil War are still found.

25

CLEBURNE'S GHOST

Another ray of light hath fled,
another Southern brave,
Hath fallen in his country's cause
and found a laureled grave—
Hath fallen, but his deathless name
shall live when stars shall set,
For, noble Cleburne, thou art one
this world will ne'er forget.
—"Cleburne" (anonymous, 1864)

They called him the Stonewall of the West. Irish by birth and southern by the grace of God, Maj. Gen. Patrick Cleburne was regarded by some as the last best hope of the Confederacy. Robert E. Lee called Cleburne "a meteor shining from a clouded sky, a young eagle in the West."

Cleburne's division was an elite force in an army renowned for its martial spirit and its incompetent commanding officer. General Hardee—one of Cleburne's peers and the man who literally wrote the book on infantry tactics—remarked that both friend and foe could easily mark the progress of Cleburne and his men in combat, by the progress of his distinctive blue battle flag, for where that flag was, there too was Cleburne. "Where this division defended, no odds broke its lines. Where it attacked, no numbers resisted the onslaught, save only once," Hardee wrote.

It has been said that Cleburne's men would have followed him to Hell and back if he had commanded them—such was their regard for him. Neither Cleburne nor his men realized that he would do exactly that on November 30, 1864.

John Bell Hood had been appointed commander of the Army of Tennessee in 1864, with the mission to counter the Federal advance into the heartland of the Confederacy. Hood proposed to do that not by defending the defenseless farmlands of Georgia and the Carolinas, but by assaulting Nashville deep behind Union lines to the North. It was already a hopeless task, but Hood brimmed with confidence—perhaps hoping to make up in audacity what he lacked in numbers. Heedless of advice to the contrary and unfamiliar with the territory, Hood set his face northward, driving his bare-foot, hungry army north towards Nashville like cattle.

Also racing towards Nashville was a Union corps under General Schofield. Nearly as large as Hood's army, Schofield had been recalled to Nashville by Gen. "Pap" Thomas, the Union commander of the district. A competition soon arose between the two forces, to see who would reach Nashville first, Schofield or Hood. At Spring Hill, Tennessee, the exhausted southern pickets failed to notice Schofield's force slip by them in the night. Schofield had "hoodwinked" his former roommate from West Point. The stage was set for a showdown at the town of Franklin the next day.

Unable to get across the last barrier to Nashville— the Harpeth River—until pontoons were brought up, Schofield ordered his rearguard to dig in near the town of Franklin and to hold off Hood until Schofield's main body could get across. Schofield's men had all day to prepare their defenses. It was not until late afternoon that Hood's main force arrived south of the town, and even then, his artillery was still far behind.

Hood ordered Cleburne and his men to lead the frontal assault at Franklin. Some say Hood wished to punish Cleburne for letting Schofield escape at Spring Hill and ordered the frontal assault by way of chastisement. It is known that when Cleburne protested the folly of the order, Hood accused him of cowardice.

It was a suicidal attack, and Cleburne knew it. His men were to charge the center of a prepared line, attacking uphill over nearly two miles of open ground. Even as they marched into battle, his men were calling it the Valley of Death.

Cleburne had never ordered his men to go any place he would not go himself, and the twilight's last gleaming found Cleburne at the head of his division, leading the attack. As he closed with the enemy, Patrick turned to one of his officers and, smiling a grim smile, said, "Well, Govan, if we are to die, let us die like men."

In the attack, Cleburne had first one, then another, horse shot out from under him, finally leading the charge on foot, waving his cap to encourage his men. That day, fifty-four regimental commanders of the Confederate army and six generals were killed or wounded in the charge. Cleburne was one of those six generals. Hood declared Franklin a Confederate victory; his men called it cold-blooded murder.

Cleburne's body was brought to Carnton mansion, home of the McGavock family. Here Cleburne was laid out on the back porch with the dead of his command stacked up like cordwood, ten deep. Throughout the evening and on into the next day, more dead and dying were brought to Carnton, which became a Confederate field hospital and morgue. Ironically, in Gaelic a Carn, or caern, is a mound erected to bury a great warrior who has died a hero's death in battle. Carnton would be the final resting place of many such men and their ghosts.

Many of Cleburne's command lie buried today at Carnton in neat rows, their name, rank, and regiment duly recorded. Row upon row they lay, a literal bivouac of the dead. Cleburne's body, however, is not with them, as his mortal remains were laid to rest elsewhere. Even if his body is long gone, there are many who swear his spirit still dwells on the grounds of Carnton.

On more than one occasion, people have heard footsteps pacing to and fro on the rear porch of the second floor. The sound of heavy boots upstairs is audible to many who visit Carnton, even though the staff do not, as a rule, mention anything of the spirits that haunt the old house. The locals commonly refer to the entity that inhabits the porch as "the general." He has been present in the house for as long as anyone can remember.

On occasion, the general has been known to make himself visible. In 1986, just before the mansion's annual fund-raiser, the Heritage Ball, a security guard's watchdog suddenly began to bark furiously at someone or something on the back side of the house. Despite the guard's repeated commands for the dog to stop, the animal kept barking.

At the rear of the building, the guard shone his flashlight around the rear porch. There, on the second story, the beam illumined the figure of a man in a long gray coat looking down at him. The guard called out to the trespasser on the upper veranda, but the man simply vanished into the dark.

In 1989, a local resident associated with the museum was driving up the majestic driveway one night, when he saw someone sitting on the back porch, leaning his head over the railing. As the car came close, the man stood up and turned to leave. The eyewitness described the apparition as having a long coat and a felt hat, yet no discernible face. The figure disappeared into the shadows; a thorough search of the house revealed no one there.

In recent years, staff members have had to remove the key from the door that leads from the hallway to the porch, which is the main entry to the back of the building. "If we leave the key in the door," a former director told a reporter, "the general locks it."

Once, local journalist Lorene Lambert interviewed Bernice Sieberling, the director of the museum at the time. As they sat in the parlor discussing the mansion's history, Lorene could hear the general prowling about on the upstairs porch, even though nothing was visible to the eye.

According to one psychic investigator, a man who stopped by the house one November at dusk has even claimed to have had a conversation with this strangely clad gentleman. The stranger mounted a horse and started to ride off into a gathering mist. The visitor said he began to suspect something was amiss when he heard the mounted stranger say as he rode off, "Well, Govan, if we are to die, let us die like men!"

Regardless of the veracity of this story, on any number of other occasions—even in broad daylight—visitors, unaware of the house's spectral reputation, have seen other gray-clad men walking about the property. Some have mistaken them for costumed reenactors, but such is not the case.

While different candidates have been proposed for the identity of the ghost which haunts the rear veranda of the Carnton, the consensus seems to be that "the general" is the spirit of Patrick Cleburne. It was Cleburne who was so close to his men; it would therefore not be unreasonable to suppose that in death, as in life, General Cleburne was looking after the welfare of his command. For there, in full view of the veranda, stand the serried gray ranks of stone that mark regiment after regiment of the dead of Cleburne's division.

General Patrick Cleburne lived with his men, he fought with his men, and he died with his men. It should come as no surprise, therefore, that Cleburne remains with his command still.

If you visit Carnton today, you will probably not hear any guide remark about the house's rich heritage of phantoms. Nor is it likely that you will see or hear anything out of the ordinary. However, if you should hear the sound of riding boots pacing on the porch, or the distant strain of "The Bonnie Blue Flag" wafting on the crisp autumn air, neither should you be too surprised.

26

PETERSBURG'S PHANTOM HOSTS

It has been said that Petersburg was the graveyard of the Confederacy. And rightly so: it is the final resting place for thirty thousand Rebel souls. For ten months, Ulysses S. Grant's well-honed war machine battered away at Robert E. Lee's outnumbered army. Open battle gave way to trench war on a scale unmatched until World War I—with all the horrors that went with it. With so much suffering and death, it is not surprising that Petersburg should play host to a number of ghosts.

Grant's goal had been the Confederate capital of Richmond, the El Dorado of all Union commanders since the start of the war. But Richmond's defenses were too strong to be taken by direct assault, so in June 1864, Grant turned southward to the rail junction at the city of Petersburg. Petersburg was the narrow bottleneck through which all supplies going to Lee and Richmond passed. Cut off that vital supply line and Richmond would be doomed, the Confederate army trapped.

Secretly, Grant moved against the strategic spot. Lee, however, with an almost sixth sense, transferred troops to that front just in time to prevent the city's capture. The Confederates beat off repeated Federal assaults in a series of desperate battles. But Grant was not like the previous Union generals Lee had fought. Instead of going away to lick his wounds, Grant hunkered down where he was, prepared to do whatever it took to win the war.

Every October, Petersburg holds ghost tours of some of its best-known haunts. On High Street, for example, stands Stewart House, one of the stops on the tour. It claims a date of 1798, but its resident revenant is vintage Civil War. There, it is said, one may see a spectral face peering from the front window. Dressed in Confederate garb, he peers at passersby, an enigmatic reminder of the war.

On a grander scale is the mansion of Centre Hill. Overlooking the Appomattox River, it was built on a magnificent scale, with a long history. A number of ghosts inhabit Centre Hill, from a "pretty lady" who dwelt on the second floor to a melodeon in the library that plays all on its own. But the most notable spectral disturbance connected with the Civil War used to occur on a set schedule.

Prior to becoming a public museum, the house's former owners found themselves unwilling hosts to a parade of phantom soldiers. Every year, on January 24, at precisely 7:30 P.M., a spectral procession took place inside the house.

First, the door to the office was heard opening, then a clatter arose like an entire regiment of soldiers tramping through the house. One could even distinguish the sound of sabers rattling in their scabbards. The phantom parade proceeded up the stairs and into a room over the office. A quarter of an hour later, the same sounds were heard in the overhead room—only this time retracing their path. Descending the stairs, the phantom regiment would cross the hallway and end their invisible procession by slamming the door. Then, all was silent once more.

All is silent at Fort Steadman as well—one of the many Federal siege works that surrounded Petersburg— but the ghosts are of a more visible sort here. Steadman was the site of one of the last major battles of the siege. In March 1865, the Rebels tried in vain to break out of the death grip that Grant had placed on the city. Nearby Fort Steadman, in the area where the Federal IX Corps once held sway, visitors to the battlefield have on occasion seen a line of Federal soldiers standing in battle array. Looking up on the hill, they seem poised to attack the Rebel lines. Yet should a viewer turn their head for but a moment, the apparitions disappear.

One park supervisor who used to live on the park property claimed he could even hear the sound of a military band playing. It was almost as regular as an alarm clock, waking him up at 5:30 A.M. daily. A small brass band played old Union airs, and the sound always seemed to come from the ridge where the Federal IX Corps had camped.

Federal phantoms are also evident elsewhere around Petersburg. Every March 31, for example, a ghost brigade can be seen marching along on White Oak Road, southwest of Petersburg. One night during the siege, a Union detachment, worn down by fatigue and constant combat, mistook a Federal column coming to relieve them for an approaching enemy force. Victims of "friendly fire," many men died that night for naught. Since that time, the phantom Federals have reappeared on the anniversary of their death, reliving their last moments.

At Petersburg, both Federals and Confederates fought to the last extremity. It would seem, in fact, that many soldiers at Petersburg have not only served to the last extremity, but to eternity as well.

27

TO THE BITTER END: BENTONVILLE

By any measure, it had been a bad winter for the Army of Tennessee. First came their Pyrrhic victory at Franklin, where the army was decimated overcoming the Yankee rearguard. That was followed only a few weeks later by the massive defeat at the Battle of Nashville. Reeling from the disastrous Tennessee campaign, the remnants of this once mighty army came straggling southward toward North Carolina.

General Hood's Nashville campaign had left the heartland of the Confederacy defenseless; everywhere, word of Sherman's barbaric behavior against the civilian population scorched the returning army's ears.

Too late, Hood was relieved of command, and Joseph E. Johnston was put in charge. Scraping together every last man he could find, Johnston resolved to make a stand in a desperate bid to halt Sherman's pillaging. The two forces met in Bentonville, North Carolina, in the last major battle of the war.

By March 1865, Johnston had managed to gather some twenty thousand men; yet he was still outnumbered more than three to one by the Yankees. There was one chance; Johnston's scouts had learned that Sherman had split his command and that one column under Maj. Gen. Henry Slocum was approaching the hamlet of Bentonville. If Johnston could engage Slocum apart from the rest of the Yankee army, he might be able to fight with something approaching a parity of numbers.

On the morning of March 19, Johnston sprung his trap. Throughout that day and on into the next, the Confederates launched attack after attack. Around the hard core of the Army of Tennessee's veterans, General Johnston had gathered old men and young boys in one last hurrah.

By the afternoon of March 20, however, two more corps of Sherman's army had arrived on the field, and the difference in numbers decided the battle against the Confederates. In the end, over four thousand men lay on the battlefield, leaving a bitter legacy of death. The Confederacy was in its death throes now, and after Bentonville everyone knew it.

The scene of North Carolina's largest Civil War battle is now preserved as a state park. Thousands of visitors come every year to experience the state's Civil War heritage. Sometimes though, the experience there is much more than just history.

In March of 1990, for example, a farmer whose land borders on the park was out cutting wood. He had his chain saw fired up and was busily at work, when suddenly his whole surroundings changed without warning. In an instant, he found himself immersed in a full-pitched battle. The acrid smell of burnt gunpowder filled his nostrils and gun smoke swirled about him in the air. He could even hear and feel bullets whizzing by, just above his head. Artillery shells began to burst all around him. The farmer flattened himself on the ground. After just a few minutes—though it seemed like an eternity—the sights and sounds of the battle ceased abruptly. The farmer did not wait for it to start up again, but instead made a dash for his pickup truck and high-tailed it out of there. It was weeks before he dared to come back for his chain saw.

Nearby, in the park proper, an old farmhouse—Harper House—is well preserved as part of the site. In March 1865, John Harper and his family found themselves in the middle of battle. The Harpers survived the ordeal, but in the wake of the duel between contending armies, the Harpers found their home turned into a hospital teeming with casualties. The Harper House is preserved much as it was back then—lacking the wounded, of course. According to some visitors, however, at least some of those casualties remain—in phantom form.

In October of the year the farmer had his battlefield encounter—a family visiting the park from Manassas, Virginia, arrived to take the tour. Instead of going to the interpretive center, where the whole story of the battle is told, they went straight to Harper House. As the group toured the place room to room, one lady in the group claimed to see a member of the Harper family in one of the rooms.

At first, their guide Jim Summerlin was confused. He asked what it was she saw. At that, the woman proceeded to give a detailed description of the apparitions in the room with them: a man with a white beard, long dark coat, and a thick set of eyebrows. Without knowing it, she had given the guide an accurate description of old man Harper, aged sixty-two!

At first, Jim was more than a little dubious of the woman's claims. But throughout the tour, the lady continued to give descriptions—with uncanny accuracy—about the people and events associated with the home. The woman even witnessed a horse-drawn ambulance pull up in front of the house and unload more casualties. Yet neither she nor her companions had any fore-knowledge of the place—not even rudimentary knowledge of the battle.

One rainy morning in 1987, a seasonal employee was busy at work in Harper House. As he was working there, all alone, he thought he heard someone moving about upstairs. Even after he came out of the back room, on the far side of Harper House, the man felt someone or something was there with him. He looked about, but no one could be seen.

Then, standing at the foot of the stairwell, the staffer caught a fleeting glimpse of something moving above him. There, he saw a dim figure at the head of the stairs. The staff worker had found himself face to face with a ghost. Jim Goode, then program coordinator of the visitors center, can still remember the sight of that part-time employee running in, all out of breath, and scared out of his wits!

Bentonville marked the death-knell of the Confederacy. It was a hopeless fight for a lost cause. Yet no men fought harder during the entire war than those soldiers fought for that day-and-a-half in North Carolina, and more than a century and a quarter later, the killing fields of Bentonville still yield a bitter harvest.

PART FIVE
THE PSYCHIC PRESIDENCY

By nature Lincoln had a temperament which bordered on the mystical. His homespun wisdom and down-to-earth humor disguised a deep-seated belief in a divinely ordered destiny which guided the course of human affairs—and America's fate in particular. That Lincoln possessed paranormal abilities is a fact which is supported by an abundance of contemporary evidence.

Lincoln also believed that it was God's will that he should become president at that particular time in history. The visions, dreams, and other omens that he experienced, or that were relayed to him, only served to confirm and reinforce his belief in destiny.

His wife, Mary Todd Lincoln, may also have had some psychic talent. For one thing, she seemed better than even Lincoln at interpreting his dreams, although they frightened and appalled her. Moreover, quite early on in their relationship, Mary Todd had set her sights on Lincoln because she had had a "presentment" of his future greatness.

28

THE MIRROR HAD
TWO FACES

It was Abraham Lincoln's own law partner, Ward Lamon, who observed that Lincoln possessed a "vision of grandeur and gloom." It was a vision that was confirmed in his mind by the dreams of his childhood, of his youthful days, and of his mature years.... Many times prior to his election to the Presidency he was both elated and alarmed by what seemed to him a rent in the veil which hides from mortal view what the future holds.

In the autumn of 1860, just after his election, Lincoln had yet another of these "visions of glory and blood," which confirmed in his mind, and in the minds of those close to him, that some destiny above that of the mortal plane was at work.

The election returns had been coming in all day, punctuated at last with a great, "Hurrah, boys!" Lincoln was both mentally and physically exhausted, and he left his campaign headquarters in Springfield to rest awhile. Throwing himself down on a lounge in his chambers, he lay opposite a bureau with a hinged mirror attached. Glancing across at the oval mirror, he noticed something strange: Lincoln saw himself reflected at nearly full length in the mirror. But his

130

face, Lincoln noted, had two separate and distinct images—the tip of the nose of one being about three inches from the tip of the other.

Lincoln was bothered—startled even—by this double image and got up to take a closer look, but it vanished. On lying down, Lincoln saw it a second time—"plainer, if possible, than before." This second time, he noticed that one of the faces was paler than the other.

Lincoln got up, and again the double image disappeared. In the excitement following the election, he put the incident out of his mind. But the thing had made a deep impression on him, and he did not forget about it. In fact, he later admitted that the vision in the mirror gave him momentary pangs of anxiety "as though something uncomfortable had happened."

A few days later, he tried the experiment again. Once more the two faces appeared to him—one his normal healthy image, the other a pallid, ghostly parody of life. After this repeat encounter, Lincoln later confided to his friends, "I never succeeded in bringing the ghost back again."

Lincoln tried to repeat the vision for the benefit of his wife, Mary, but to no avail. Nevertheless, it was Mary who seemed to grasp the full import of this vision—and grew quite worried as a result. Though Mary never made claim to any particular psychic abilities, she seemed, more than anyone, to have a knack for interpreting Lincoln's dreams and visions.

It was clearly a sign, she told her husband, that he would be elected to a second term in office. But the upsetting part to her was the deathly pallor of the second face, which she said indicated that he would die before the end of his second term in office.

As he often did with such things, Lincoln tried to make light of the vision to Mary, to avoid worrying

Mary unduly. He laughed it off as just an odd optical illusion. But he clearly did not believe that, any more than she did.

The "double vision" on the night of his elevation to the highest political office in the land, in a time of unprecedented upheavals, could not fail to impress Lincoln as a sign of utmost importance.

The incident confirmed his long-held belief that he had a special destiny to fulfill. That the omen also foretold his own death, and that despite it, he still proceeded on his chosen course, is a testament to Lincoln's moral courage.

29

OF A SHIP SAILING RAPIDLY: THE FINAL VISIONS OF ABRAHAM LINCOLN

"Here, Captain! dear father!
This arm beneath your head!
It is some dream that on the deck
You've fallen cold and dead...
—Walt Whitman, "O Captain! My Captain!"

April 14, 1865, was an important day in many respects. Not only was it Good Friday, the day Jesus was crucified by his enemies, it was a politically important day in Washington, D.C. Richmond had fallen, Robert E. Lee had surrendered, and events elsewhere were moving rapidly toward a conclusion.

It was against this backdrop that Lincoln's War Cabinet met on the morning of April 14. Lincoln, Seward, Stanton, Welles, and the rest of the Cabinet were all present that morning, and the guest of honor was none other than Ulysses S. Grant, there to tell them personally the details of the surrender of Lee and his army.

Initially, discussion had centered on problems inherent in the demobilizing of the huge Federal army once the last fires of the rebellion had been stamped out. Inevitably, though, the conversation turned to General Sherman and his army down in North Carolina.

No news had been heard from Sherman for some days, and with wily Joe Johnston's Confederate army still on the loose, there was still some apprehension about danger from that quarter. Lincoln, however, seemed quite optimistic—uncharacteristically so.

With a heavy burden on his shoulders, Lincoln could sometimes be very morose in private, and many cabinet meetings during the war had been somber affairs as well. But now, Lincoln seemed positively buoyant with optimism.

"We shall hear very soon, and the news will be important," Lincoln told them.

General Grant, wondering what source the president had drawn on for his intelligence, asked Lincoln why he thought this so.

"Because," replied Lincoln, "I had a dream last night; and ever since this war began I have had the same dream just before every event of national importance. It portends some important event that will happen very soon. I seemed to be in a singular and indescribable vessel, but always the same, and to be moving with great rapidity toward a dark and indefinite shore."

The cabinet and the general were listening in rapt attention as Lincoln continued. "I have had this singular dream preceding the firing on Sumter, the Battles of Bull Run, Antietam, Gettysburg, Stone's River, Vicksburg, Wilmington, and the like."

At this point, Grant, the hard-headed realist, pointed out that Lincoln's list included Stone's River and that he did not consider Stone's River a Union victory.

"I don't altogether agree with you," said Lincoln with regard to the status of Stone's River, "but whatever the facts, my singular dream preceded that fight. Victory has not always followed my dream, but the event and the results have been important."

Lincoln interpreted the latest recurrence of his dream as a sign that Sherman had vanquished Johnston in the Carolinas because the president's thoughts were in that direction. "I know of no other very important event which is likely just now to occur."

They say that no man knows the hour of his death, not even a prophet. So it was with Lincoln. He could not—would not—see that the great event his dream forewarned of was his own assassination. Yet, just a few days prior to this dream, Lincoln had had another dream that spoke even more clearly to him of his fate.

A few days prior to the April 14 meeting, Lincoln had told his wife Mary and his close friend and confidante Ward Lamon of a most chilling dream he had had some days before.

"About ten days ago," Lincoln said, "I retired very late. I had been up waiting for an important dispatch from the front. I could not have been long in bed when I fell into a slumber, for I was weary. I soon began to dream. There seemed to be a deathlike stillness about me. Then I heard subdued sobs, as if a number of people were weeping. I thought I left my bed and wandered downstairs. There the silence was broken by the same pitiful sobbing, but the mourners were invisible. I went from room to room; no living person was in sight, but the same mournful sounds of distress met me as I passed along. It was light in all the rooms; every object was familiar to me; but where were all the people who were grieving as if their hearts would break?

"Determined to find the cause of a state of things so mysterious and so shocking, I kept on until I arrived at the East Room, which I entered. There I met with a sickening surprise. Before me was a catafalque on which rested a corpse wrapped in funeral vestments. Around it were stationed soldiers who were acting as guards; and there was a throng of people, some gazing mournfully upon the corpse, whose face was covered, others weeping pitifully. 'Who is dead in the White House?' I demanded of one of the soldiers. 'The President,' was his answer. 'He was killed by an assassin!' Then came a loud burst of grief from the crowd, which awoke me from my dream."

Lincoln had been profoundly disturbed by this grim vision. The President could sleep no more that night, and opened the Bible for consolation. Yet, every passage in both the Old and New Testaments to which he turned made reference to dreams, visions, or other omens. It was almost as if providence wished to drive home the meaning of the dream he had just been given.

Interestingly enough, Lincoln was not the only one in Washington experiencing premonitions that day. The same morning of the Cabinet meeting, Julia Grant had had her own presentment of sorts. No sooner had they awoken that morning, than Mrs. Grant urgently entreated her husband that they leave Washington that day.

With the war winding down, they had been planning to leave for Burlington, New Jersey, as soon as the general's duties would permit. Yet, there had not been any real urgency to the matter. But on that morning, Julia was filled with an inexplicable urge to leave town immediately.

Because the Cabinet meeting had been moved from 9 A.M. to 11 A.M., the general told his wife it would probably prevent their leaving that evening. This made Julia all the more insistent that they leave town—and leave that very day.

Later that day, Mrs. Grant received an invitation for her and Ulysses to attend a play at Ford's Theatre that night with the president and Mrs. Lincoln. Julia, rather than being flattered, in her own words, "took a freak" at the prospect. She could not explain it, even to herself. But it was a feeling she could neither ignore nor resist. Julia immediately shot off a note to her husband, pleading with him to come home; that she did not want to go to the theater; that he must take her home to Burlington, New Jersey.

Not only did she write her husband, but when three staff officers stopped by to pay their respects, she dragooned them into conveying her repeated entreaty to her husband! That afternoon, as the Grants rode their carriage to the railway station, a stranger on a black horse shadowed them, further reinforcing Julia Grant's apprehension over staying in town that evening.

The general and his wife arrived at Philadelphia without incident. It was there, however, that word reached them of Lincoln's assassination in Washington and the attempts made on the lives of several of the Cabinet members.

All that day, a nameless dread had fallen upon Julia Grant, an overwhelming apprehension she could not rationally explain. All she knew was that she and her husband must not remain in the city that night—and under no circumstances go the theater!

Once more, one of Julia Grant's "singular visions" had been correct. There was some evidence that came to light later—though never publicized—that Grant had been targeted for assassination as well that night. Another assassin, never caught, was detailed by John Wilkes Booth to kill Grant and so make a clean sweep of the Yankee government.

Then it came to pass that the "ship of state" arrived safely at its destination, though its captain died just before reaching the dark and distant shore. The country would never be the same again. The circumstances surrounding the assassination of Abraham Lincoln remain shrouded in mystery to this day. But there is little doubt that some agency beyond mortal ken was at work in the days and hours leading up to Lincoln's assassination.

That this unseen agency was seeking to warn Lincoln of his impending doom is clear, and was clear even to those closer in time and proximity to the president. So it was that Mary Todd Lincoln's first words on realizing her husband had been shot were, "His dream was prophetic."

Prophetic indeed.

30

LINCOLN'S
FAVORITE HAUNTS

C ertainly no figure from the Civil War is more closely associated with the supernatural than Abraham Lincoln. In life, Lincoln was the center of many strange and uncanny occurrences. In death, the Great Emancipator is still a nexus for the supernatural.

The ghost of Abraham Lincoln, in fact, has been reported at a number of different locations. So much so, in fact, it gives one pause to wonder at what historic site does Lincoln's ghost not dwell. Foremost of all the places that Lincoln's shade is known to inhabit is, of course, the White House.

By all accounts, nearly every administration since Lincoln's has had some sort of spectral encounter with Lincoln's ghost. White House staff, visiting dignitaries, as well as presidents and their wives have all had a brush with the supernatural while residing there.

Teddy Roosevelt hinted at having an encounter with the Rail-Splitter from Illinois. President Calvin Coolidge's wife, Grace, swore that Lincoln materialized before her eyes, dressed in black, with a shawl or stole draped over his shoulder to ward off the night air.

During FDR's historic administration, a number of prominent people were visited by the ghost of Lincoln.

Eleanor Roosevelt never actually saw him—but she definitely felt his presence there.

One day, however, one of the Roosevelts' housekeepers—Mary Evan—was passing by the Lincoln bedroom. Glancing in, she saw a tall, gaunt figure pulling on his boots. She was certain it was the ghost of Lincoln. She ran screaming down the stairs in the White House.

Other servants, including some Secret Service agents, have sighted Lincoln roaming the hallways and various rooms of the White House.

There is a tradition associated with the White House, that Abraham Lincoln appears there only in times of national emergency, or when the current president is under great stress. This theory may explain the cluster of Lincoln sightings at the White House during World War II.

Exiled Queen Wilhelmina of Holland, for example, stayed briefly in the White House's Rose Room during the second World War. She was in the bedroom late at night, when she heard a knock at the door. She opened the door, and there before her stood the lanky figure of Lincoln. The Queen fainted dead away, coming to on the floor of the Rose Room.

Winston Churchill also stayed at the White House during the war on several occasions. He was always uncomfortable sleeping in the Lincoln Room, which had been Lincoln's office during the Civil War. As often as not, Winston would move to another room rather than stay the night there.

Harry Truman, who was the first president to have to deal with the Cold War, was quite sure that the White House was haunted. "Give 'em Hell Harry" however, claimed he was not afraid of any resident spooks, so much as "the live nuts I have to see every day!"

One night, Truman was awakened by two loud knocks on his bedroom door. He went to the door, but no one was there—just a chilled feeling and the faint sound of footsteps trailing away.

In the 1960s, Lynda Bird Johnson, Lyndon Johnson's daughter, was also awakened by a phantom knocker, with similar results. More recently, in the 1980s, Reagan family members seem to have had a number of incidents during their stay in the presidential mansion. Maureen Reagan apparently saw Lincoln during her and her husband's stay in the Lincoln Room, for one thing.

While Nancy Reagan—the queen of spin—has denied any spectral encounters, the Great Communicator has been more forthcoming about the presence of the Great Emancipator in the White House. While Reagan never actually saw the ghost of Lincoln, his dog Rex would often start down the hall, stalking some unseen presence and barking furiously. Rex would bark and bark at the threshold to the Lincoln Room, but would not go into the room itself. Rex would then back away, growling, when Reagan tried to have him enter the room.

Talking to a group of students on Lincoln's birthday in 1987, Reagan expressed no fear of Honest Abe's specter. Reagan felt it would be "wonderful" to have a meeting with Lincoln—"and probably very helpful," he told the students.

So great a spirit as Lincoln's, of course, cannot be confined to just one place. Fortress Monroe, for example, standing astride Chesapeake Bay like a stony sentinel, played host to Lincoln during the war—and still does, by all accounts.

While at Fortress Monroe, Lincoln would always stay in the commandant's quarters—"Old Quarters

Number One"—and in recent times, Lincoln has been sighted in one particular room of those quarters—the Lincoln Room. This suite is named after him because it was precisely the room he stayed at when he visited during the war. He has been seen in the Lincoln Room, standing by the fireplace and clothed in a dressing gown. Many who have seen Lincoln's ghost there say he seems engrossed in deep thought.

In Lincoln's hometown of Springfield, Illinois, the Lincoln Home, now a national historic site, has also been the scene of many sightings over the years. National Park Service bureaucrats, of course, issue the usual flat denial that the house is haunted, but numerous visitors and even some former parks service employees tell a different tale.

Folks touring the Lincoln home in Springfield have claimed to see a young boy by Lincoln's side; it is believed to be his son Willie, who died while Lincoln was serving as president, and whose body was reinterred with Lincoln after his assassination.

Former employees have had the sensation of someone touching them on the shoulder, only to turn around and find no one there. At other times, parks department staff have seen the Great Emancipator's rocking chair begin to rock all on its own.

At nearby Oak Ridge Cemetery, the tomb of Lincoln stands as permanent shrine to the martyred president. Since Lincoln and his son Willie were laid to rest there, visitors—and occasional tomb robbers—have come by the thousands to pay homage. Some of these folk have reported strange sounds coming from the steps of the tomb at night. The sounds of footsteps, and a sobbing sound, seem the most common occurrences. Some locals have even claimed to see his familiar silhouette wandering the grounds around the tomb at midnight.

The skeptical may well ask how you can be at three different places, when you're not anywhere at all. If one accepts the notion that the soul survives death, and is thenceforth not bound by the laws of material existence, it follows that so long as it has nothing to hold it to one spot or another, then what the mind can picture, the spirit can experience.

For the dead, it would seem, there is only the eternal now, and those places most bound up with memories of life—and death—would naturally be focal points for a post-mortem consciousness.

The night Lincoln passed, Secretary of War Stanton was heard to exclaim "He belongs to the Ages, now." In far more than one sense, that has proved true to this day.

31

THE RESTLESS
WRAITHS OF LINCOLN'S
ASSASSINS

The facts surrounding the psychic presidency are
well documented. But what of those foul souls who
murdered him? Are their spirits at peace, or are they
cursed for all eternity? Are the assassins, in fact,
doomed to relive their black deeds through eternity?

Spectral sightings of those connected with the Lincoln assassination have been reported in a number of
locations with uncanny regularity around the Washington, D.C., area.

The 'unindicted co-conspirator,' John Wilkes Booth,
though, seems to be surprisingly little in evidence. One
place that does seem to retain some psychic memory of
his fatal act is Ford's Theater in Washington.

Tradition has it, that any actor attempting to deliver
his lines at any spot along the escape route Booth took
across the stage of Ford's is doomed to flub or forget
them. Moreover, when all is deathly quiet in the old
theater, Booth's heavy footsteps can still be heard,
echoing throughout the halls of the theater.

Since the Ford's Theater's reopening in 1968, moreover, both actors and work-crews have reported spectral

encounters with the actual ghost of John Wilkes Booth after hours. Some ham actors, it would seem, just cannot stand to leave the stage.

Supernatural phenomena have also been reported at the scene of Booth's death, the Garrett Farm. After he was shot in the burning barn of the farm, the dying Booth breathed his last on the nearby porch of the Garrett family farmhouse.

Booth's blood oozed onto the boards of the porch, staining it with a large crimson splotch, and though the family tried to bleach the stain out, local folk have told how it would return every time it rained. The Garretts finally wearied of trying to erase the bloody splotch— desperate to rid themselves of Booth's continuing presence in their midst—and finally tore up all the boards of the porch.

Perhaps the most tragic figure of the whole sordid affair was Mary Surratt, the woman whose boarding house Booth had used as his headquarters for planning the assassination. Although Mary's son, John, was one of the conspirators, there was never any direct evidence that Mary herself knew of the plot. Yet the administration, thirsting for blood, had the old widow arrested, tried, and on July 7, 1865, was hanged along with the rest of the assassins. She was the first woman ever executed in American history.

Mary Surratt's spirit, it is said, still lingers on, in the hope of being vindicated. The Surratt Boarding House in Washington, D.C., quickly became an ill-omened place. Surratt's daughter Annie, sold it off cheaply; but successive owners reported strange sounds emanating from within its walls.

Over the years, residents at the house at 604 H Street in Washington, claimed to hear strange mumbling sounds like muffled voices. Some of the voices were clear enough at times to make out individual voices, and it sounded to some ears like several men working out the details of a conspiracy to commit murder. At other times, however, one could hear lighter footsteps, pacing to and fro in the former bedroom of Mary Surratt. The sites where she was imprisoned and executed are also reputed to be imbued with the phantom landlady's presence.

Mary Surratt was initially incarcerated at the Old Capitol Prison, an old government office converted to penal use. While it stood, the Old Prison was visited by the ghost of Mrs. Surratt every year on the anniversary of her death—her silhouette being seen in one of the cell windows for years. The Old Capitol Prison was torn down some years back, to make way for the Supreme Court building in Washington.

After a brief show trial that would have made Robespierre proud, Mrs. Surratt was condemned to death. After her conviction, she and the other conspirators were transferred to the Old Arsenal Prison, which lay nearby, on the Anacostia River. Today, it is the site of a modern military base, Fort McNair. Over the years, a number of military personnel at Fort McNair have noticed strange things occur in the areas of the base connected with Mrs. Surratt and the conspirators. Soon after the execution of Mrs. Surratt, a boxwood tree sprang up spontaneously on the spot of her hanging. It was widely interpreted at the time, that her execution was unjust.

More recently, when a major snowstorm hit the Washington, D.C., area, and the area was blanketed with a foot-thick layer of snow, on the parade ground where the old prison yard had once been, a cleared path appeared, some 300 yards long. The cleared path was the precise route the condemned had taken the morning of their execution. No one on the base had cleared the snow away, and a careful check of camp blueprints proved there were no underground pipes or heating conduits that could have caused so much snow to melt on its own. Nor was that the only strange phenomenon associated with Mrs. Surratt and her imprisonment there. One army officer at Fort McNair, on Lincoln's birthday, heard the voice of a woman outside his window, alternately pleading softly for help and screaming. On another occasion, a lieutenant saw the ghost of a stout, older woman, clothed darkly, floating through the halls of the officers' quarters. A major's wife had a similar encounter.

Residents of Quarters 20 on the base seem to have had the most experience with the supernatural. Hammering, sawing, and other odd noises can be heard from that apartment. At night, a drumming sound is reported. In Quarters 20, objects have been seen to move all on their own—everything from pool balls to flower pots have been tossed about! As it turns out, Quarters 20 is built right over the spot where Mary Surratt was held while awaiting her execution.

In nearby Maryland, about thirteen miles from Washington, on Brandywine Road in Prince George County, stands an old home. At the time of Lincoln's assassination, it was leased to a former police officer, John Lloyd, who ran a tavern there; but it still belonged to the widow Surratt. It was largely Lloyd's perjured testimony that led to Mary Surratt's conviction.

In the 1940s a number of people reported seeing the ghost of Mary Surratt on the stairway of the old tavern. Others claimed to hear men's voices engaged in conversation in the back of the house; no one was ever seen in the back of the house—but a man in dark clothes was sighted on the front porch.

Since 1965, the Surratt Tavern has been open to the public as a historic site, run by the state of Maryland. Since its opening to the public at large, if anything, the number of strange occurrences and sightings have increased.

Museum staff have heard the sound of footsteps in the upstairs hallway, with no one there. The distinct aroma of tobacco smoke has also been noted by both visitors and staff, even though nobody is smoking, while the facial expressions on the portrait of Mary Surratt have been observed to change at various times, and the eyes seem to follow you around the room.

A male presence definitely seems to reside in the house, in addition to that of Mary Surratt. Could it be the ghost of John Lloyd, unable to find rest in death, for the lies he told in life?

If Mary Surratt's guilt is far from clear, the case of Doctor Mudd is murkier still. While most historians regard Mudd as an innocent victim of a vindictive military tribunal, the evidence is equivocal. Doctor Samuel A. Mudd, a Confederate sympathizer, claimed not to recognize John Wilkes Booth the night he treated his broken leg.

Yet Mudd also admitted that he had known the actor-turned-assassin well before that fatal night. The suspicion remains that Mudd may have been an accomplice to the conspiracy, and that Mudd's Maryland farmhouse was intended to be used as a safe house by the conspirators.

Over several generations, the doctor's family has tried to clean the besmirched Mudd name, and have steadfastly maintained his innocence. Apparently, the good doctor himself has had input in this regard.

In the 1960s, a granddaughter of Doctor Mudd, Louise Mudd Arehart, began experiencing strange incidents at her home in La Plata, Maryland. Knockings on her front door, and finding no one there, plus other strange noises, began to become commonplace for Louise.

Soon Louise began to see a strange man, dressed in black, on her property. Finally, he began to appear inside her home, even passing her in the hallway. but he would always vanish without a trace. Mrs. Arehart even led her dog through the house to sniff out any mortal intruder—to no avail.

The stranger's face was vaguely familiar to Louise. Then one day, it struck her—that mysterious stranger was her grandfather, Dr. Samuel Mudd! Louise began to piece together the solution of the mysterious visitations.

The ancestral home of the Mudds had remained in the family, but over the course of several decades had gradually fallen victim to neglect. Mrs. Arehart realized that her grandfather wished the home restored and opened to the public, so that his side of the story could be better known. Though the doctor had finally been pardoned, the soil on the good name of Mudd remained.

Mobilizing relatives, and garnering public support, the Mudd house was restored, placed on the National Register of Historic Places, and finally opened to the public. Then, in the 1970s, former President Jimmy Carter publicly proclaimed the doctor's innocence.

Perhaps because of all these positive developments, grandpa Mudd has been considerably less in evidence. Of all the restless revenants associated with the assassination of Lincoln, Doctor Mudd seems to have been the only one to have attained his purpose.

The old Ford's Theater has been renovated and restored for many years now, and is open for both tours and performances; contact: Ford's Theater, 511 Tenth St. NW, Washington, DC, 20004, (202) 347-4833.

For those curious about Mrs. Surratt and her fate, the best place to start would be Surratt House: Surratt House Museum, P.O. Box 427, 9118 Brandywine Road, Clinton, MD 20735, (301) 868-1121.

32

THE WESTBOUND
TRAIN GOING HOME

The nation was in a state of shock. Out of the blue their leader had been cut down in full view of a large crowd. His wife, sitting beside him, could only watch in horror as the fatal bullet struck him in the head. As president, he had led the nation through a turbulent time, and now he was cut down in his prime.

Anyone who came of age in the 1960s can tell you exactly when and where they were when they heard the news of Kennedy's assassination on November 22, 1963. They can remember, too, the sense of collective grief and trauma that the whole nation experienced as it witnessed the spectacle of his body's return to Washington, D.C., and burial.

Only those to whom that event remains a living memory can begin to grasp what the American people went through as news spread of the assassination of Abraham Lincoln on April 14, 1865. America is still living with the consequences of both events. Shocked and appalled at the incident, even Lincoln's old political enemies mourned his passing, paying their respects to him along with thousands of others as he lay in state in the Capitol.

In that era, the majority of the nation could not participate in the formal ceremonies being held in Washington, D.C. When the time came to transport the slain president's body back home, therefore, a special train was assembled, that would take Lincoln's mortal remains by a roundabout route to Illinois, so the people might view their leader for the last time.

At 8 A.M., on April 21, 1865, Lincoln's funeral train left Washington, beginning its 1,654-mile odyssey through the heartland of America to Springfield, Illinois.

Lincoln's body reposed in a special parlor car, luxuriously appointed and of extraordinary size. It had been specially built for the President's use while traveling. Ironically, the first and only time Lincoln was to travel in it was on the way to the grave.

The other cars of the train carried three hundred mourners, plus a military Guard of Honor. The only member of the family to accompany the body was Robert Lincoln, oldest son; Mrs. Lincoln was too distraught to make the journey, and remained in Washington.

As the train chugged its way northward, one could see above the cow-catcher of the engine a framed picture of Lincoln. Along the side of the cars, garlands of black crepe proclaimed this a funeral train.

Baltimore, Harrisburg, Philadelphia, New York— the miles slowly passed. In each city, mourners by the tens of thousands, and then the hundreds of thousands, filed past to view their slain leader. From New York City, the train wound its way up the Hudson River Valley through dozens of small communities. In each town, throngs lined the rails to catch a glimpse of the train. After being viewed overnight by the citizens of Albany, the train headed westward toward Buffalo, through Ohio and Indiana, and on to Chicago.

In each small town along the way, by night or in the day, people came to view the train as it passed. Veterans gave a salute with their one good arm, women wept rivers of tears and the children stood in silent awe at the spectacle. In Richmond, Indiana, alone, for example, some fifteen thousand turned out as the train passed by at three in the morning—more than the entire population of the city.

On the morning of May 3, the funeral train arrived at last in Springfield, Lincoln's hometown. Here, too, the people were given a chance to view Lincoln one last time, lying in state in the very hall where he had once delivered his now famous "House Divided" speech. Then, with great and somber pomp, the president was laid to rest in Oak Ridge Cemetery.

The funeral train had arrived at its destination and delivered its cargo; the journey was at an end—or was it? In the years since, reports have surfaced of people sighting a westbound train on the anniversary of Lincoln's passing.

This is no ordinary train. Its old-fashioned engine and antique cars mark it out as unusual, if not positively bizarre. It seems gliding along through a cornfield, where the tracks were long ago taken up. And the places where it has been spotted have been known to vary. But all agree on one thing; they are certain this train is the Phantom Funeral Train of Abraham Lincoln.

When and where the report of the Phantom Funeral Train first surfaced is difficult to pinpoint. Such things usually are. I first heard of it from my father's lips when I was a child growing up. He placed the ghostly visitation in upstate New York. My father had never seen the Phantom Train, but his father—Augustus W. "Pop Gus" Coleman—had been an engineer for the railroads, driving freight trains for many years in the Hudson River Valley and upstate New York.

By all accounts, "Pop Gus" had many a tale to tell—when he could ever get a word in edgewise among all the womenfolk. No doubt, many an old railroad man could tell a similar tale.

As I have heard it, the Phantom Funeral Train appears along the old right of way in upstate New York, retracing its fateful journey. It always appears at night—some say midnight—and always on the anniversary of Lincoln's death. The train is complete in every detail, they say; the old steam engine puffing along with its flared funnel; the black-creped passage cars; and the funeral coach itself.

A band can be seen playing a dirge but no sound greets the ear; it is music only the dead can hear. And if there be any doubt about the true nature of the train, a closer look at the band reveals the truth; it consists of skeletons, still clad in their military uniforms of midnight blue, playing their instruments as they did in life.

The spectacle, they say, lasts but a moment or two; but for those who witness it, time seems to stand still. Farmers through whose wheat fields the old right of way runs, shun that place on such nights.

There are scattered reports of similar sightings elsewhere besides New York; Ohio, Indiana, and the like. Many are fragmentary, casual accounts, hard to verify. But all of them seem to report the same strange phenomena and all are along the route of the original Funeral Train. Can all these reports be fantasy or folklore?

Serious investigators of the paranormal believe that many authentic hauntings are not the spirits of the dead per se. Rather, many such incidents, especially those that mechanically repeat a specific—usually traumatic—event are actually a kind of psychic imprint. Somehow, the intense emotions surrounding a tragic incident have a residual effect, and the memory of that trauma becomes in some manner etched into the fabric of time and space.

Certainly, the overwhelming collective sense of loss and grief that was expressed by tens of thousands of mourners as they watched that Funeral Train pass by in April, 1865, would qualify as a sufficiently powerful force to create such an effect.

In the early hours of April 15, 1865, Abraham Lincoln was pronounced dead by physicians; he had "gone west" as they used to say. Since that time, the Phantom Funeral Train has continued to "go west". Perhaps someday, they too, will reach their final destination.

PART SIX
IN THE WAKE
OF THE TEMPEST

Every tempest has its ending, no matter how long it lasts or how terrible the destruction it has wrought. So too was it with the Civil War. A nation that had gone to war with itself so gaily to start with, only a short span of years later was now weary of sacrifice and pain.

For some, of course, there would be no homecoming; for others, it was much delayed. One way or another the end came to all, and in the end—as with all storms—a rainbow appeared to point the way to a brighter day for all.

33

THE LAST PRISONER

Long after all the other prisoners of war had been released and sent home, he remained. Weighed down with shackles of iron, and locked deep within stone and steel in a dank dungeon cell, he was held in durance vile.

The radical Republicans accused him of complicity in Lincoln's assassination but could not produce a shred of evidence to support their accusation. No matter; they would have put him on trial for treason, yet feared he might somehow get a fair trial by mistake, and prove his innocence. So there he stayed, behind heavy padlocked doors, the last prisoner of war—Jefferson Davis.

Fort Monroe has a long history, and over the course of its use as a military base have grown many tales of hauntings—including that of Jefferson Davis and his wife, Varina. Sitting securely in Chesapeake Bay, Fort Monroe has long had the repute of being unassailable, and throughout the war it did remain securely in Union hands, even though it sat on Virginia soil.

So, when the Yankees finally hunted Jefferson Davis down and hauled him away, it was to Fort Monroe they took him. Locked away in this stout fortress, in Casemate No. 2, not only was it impossible for the former Confederate president to break out; no one could possibly break in to free him either.

Not content with shutting Davis within tons of stone and steel, the Federal authorities shackled Davis hand and foot. His health began to decline, as a result, to the point where even the Yankee doctors became concerned. Through it all, Davis' wife Varina fought with all her might to liberate him and improve his conditions at Fort Monroe.

Finally, the government relented and placed him in less austere confinement at the fort—though still a prisoner—and his family were allowed to stay in quarters on the island. Through it all, Varina never wavered in her loyalty to her husband. The Cause may have been lost, but Varina would never give up on her 'Jeffie'.

At last, in 1867, Davis was set free, with no charges ever brought against him. To some, Jefferson Davis became a symbol for the injustices of Reconstruction. But for Davis and his family, active politics was a thing of the past. Broken in body and spirit, he left prison to write his memoirs and enjoy what was left of his life. In the end, only death brought Jefferson Davis any real peace—or did it?

At Fort Monroe, it is Varina's ghost that is said to be most evident. In the quarters directly opposite the casemate dungeon where her Jeffie had been thrown, Varina has often been seen in a second floor window.

Still used as quarters by army personnel, the room where Varina once stayed is now a bedroom in the officers' quarters. Early one morning, an army wife staying in that apartment awoke to see the figure of a grown woman and a little girl standing in the room, gazing out the window.

Startled, the wife jumped out of bed and moved towards the two intruders. The woman reached to touch the hoop skirt of the mother, but as she did, the image dissolved before her eyes. This same window also has a certain peculiarity that other military staff have observed; the window has a habit of vibrating all on its own. One resident of the quarters described it as sounding like a mechanical vibrator—sometimes so loud it drowns out the television.

The vibrating window generally starts at four in the afternoon, and continues on until late in the evening. Army personnel have tried to wedge it shut with no success. Varina's window is the only one in the old building to perform that odd trick; and coincidentally, it is the only window in direct line of sight to the cell where Jefferson Davis had been imprisoned.

Jefferson Davis' ghost has also been spotted at Fort Monroe—though not, interestingly enough, in the case-mate dungeon. It so happens that late at night some-times, the tall thin figure of Davis has been sighted pacing the ramparts, or Terraplain, of Fort Monroe, generally wandering past the area of the flagstaff along the top of a massive stone wall. It may be that, while imprisoned there deep within the fort's bowels, in his mind Davis imagined walking freely along the ram-parts above, breathing in the fresh sea breezes. In death, his spirit is free to do what was denied it in life.

In Mississippi, along the Gulf Coast, stands Beau-voir, the last home of Davis and his wife. It was here Jefferson Davis came after wandering the globe in exile for ten years; it was here he set down his memoirs of his presidency of the Confederacy; and it was here he realized a brief span of peace before he died.

By all accounts, both Jeff and Varina continue to dwell here. On rare occasion, people have seen their apparitions; mostly though, they make their presence felt in more subtle ways. One of the busts in the home has been reported to shed tears, and people walking the grounds will encounter cold spots even on the hottest August day. In the outbuildings, security guards sometimes see old men clad in gray—the ghosts of Confederate veterans who lived there after Davis died, when the place was converted to a retirement home for elderly Rebels.

To judge from accounts of Jefferson Davis' life—and afterlife—it would seem that the last leader of the Lost Cause, is in many ways still held captive—by the memories of the war and its aftermath.

Fort Monroe is still an active army base, but they do have a museum that is open to the public: The Casemate Museum, P.O. Box 5134, Casemate 20, Bernard Road, Fort Monroe, VA 23451, (757) 727-3973.

In Mississippi, Beauvoir is operated by the Mississippi Division of the Sons of Confederate Veterans and is open to the public: Beauvoir, 2244 Beach Boulevard, Biloxi, MS 39531, (228) 388-1313.

34

THE WIDOW'S WALK

High on a bluff overlooking the Cumberland, stands the city of Clarksville. Among the quaint old homes that line its quiet streets is a place they call the Smith-Trahern House. It stands in gaunt splendor next to the old city cemetery on McClure Street. Originally built by Christopher Smith in the 1850s, it was renovated by a local resident—Joseph Trahern—in the late 1940s.

In its day, the old house was called the "Queen of the Cumberland" with every modern convenience one could imagine in the 1850s—a majestic winding staircase, doubled living rooms, a parlor, and even indoor plumbing. The owner—"Kit" Smith—went to great lengths to make sure his beautiful young bride, Lucy Dabney Smith, had every convenience that money could buy; for Kit was a wealthy man.

Montgomery and Robertson counties were Tobacco Country, and after farmers had cured their bright leaf into dark-fired gold, they would haul it into Clarksville by wagon along the old buffalo trails now widened to wagon roads, or else by flatboat down the serpentine Red River, which bled into the Cumberland at that point. As one of the leading tobacco merchants of the region, Kit would buy their dark-fired leaf and then have it shipped downriver on the paddle-wheel steamboats that would tie up on the riverbank below the bluffs.

Smith was often away on business trips downriver, seeking to obtain the best terms possible for his leaf in Memphis, Natchez or New Orleans. His young bride pined for him on those occasions, wishing to be the first to catch a glimpse of his steamboat.

In order to humor his loving bride's desires, Kit had a Widow's Walk built on the roof of their home. Such a feature was not common in the mid-South. It was a feature originally designed for the wives of New England sea captains, whose husbands were oft at sea. They would pace the rooftop walkway to while away the days till their man would return to port. Like Kit's bride, they wanted to be the first one to catch a glimpse of his top-gallants on the horizon.

Sadly, many times the Yankee wives would pace in vain, for their man and his ship had been lost at sea—hence the origin of the wooden walkway's morbid nickname. Of course, Kit's bride had little to worry on that score—he had never been to sea, and had no intention of doing so now; just tedious business trips downriver on ornate paddle-wheel steamers. A few weeks routine journey, was all.

Life was as pleasant as it can be for a pair of newly-weds in a Tennessee border-town like Clarksville. Or rather, it was, until the War broke out. Whatever Kit's sympathies were in the conflict, it was quite plain that the war was bad for business. Normal trade routes were interrupted, with boats being commandeered, and crops stolen or destroyed by both sides at random. Confederate greenbacks or Yankee script, it was all the same to Smith—just a form of legalized thievery.

It was therefore something of a relief when news came in July of 1863 that Vicksburg and Port Hudson had fallen, in Mississippi and Louisiana respectively. While Kit may have regretted the double loss to the cause, business was business, and he knew the twin victories would mean that soon the entire length of the Mississippi, Ohio, and Cumberland Rivers would soon be open to free navigation again. It was only a matter of time before trade would return to normal. Smith and his wife could now look forward to an end to their financial difficulties.

With the Mississippi unvexed, Smith began to reestablish his business connections downriver, but it was not easy. Finally, as the war was winding down, Smith felt the need for a trip all the way to New Orleans to secure major new outlets for his goods. It was an important trip, he told Lucy, but it would not last long—a few weeks at most.

After obtaining the necessary passes and other papers from Federal authorities, Kit Smith made his good-byes to his beloved, and boarded a packet boat headed downstream.

Weeks passed, and every day Mrs. Smith would ascend the steep stairs to the upper deck, there to gaze out beyond the wrought iron railing that bounded the walk. Gazing out over the rooftops, Lucy scanned the bend of the river for those faint puffs of steam that would tell her that her husband's boat was coming.

Day after day, she stood on the widow's walk, a solitary figure, staring out into the distance. At long last, word arrived from downriver: Kit Smith would not be coming home—not now, not ever.

The folks in Clarksville never did get a clear story about how Kit actually died; some said he died of Yellow Fever in New Orleans. Others held that Kit had been in a hurry to get home after his business had been concluded, and that Kit booked passage aboard the first boat headed northward. The once luxurious steamboat was packed to the rafters with Yankee soldiers, men just released from prison-camps, and like Kit, eager to return home. The side-wheeler was unfit for navigation with such a heavy human cargo, but in the tumult and chaos of the war's final days, nobody much cared.

As it was chugging up the big river, the steamer's boilers started becoming overloaded. The safety valve jammed, and as the gauge entered the red zone, the boilers went critical and exploded with a tremendous blinding flash. No artillery barrage during the war could have done as much damage in so short a time; within seconds the whole ship was a blazing inferno, and the ship went down with terrible loss of life. Kit Smith's body was never found.

Now, the rooftop promenade of the Smith house earned well its sobriquet. Lucy Smith continued to climb the stairs as she had done, day after day. Lucy was no longer clad all in white; rather, she now was garbed all in black from head to toe. People became used to seeing her there, a mournful, lonely figure standing vigil on the widow's walk. What was it that she was looking for, people wondered; was she hoping for the impossible?

After many years of pining and grieving in this fashion, in 1905, Lucy passed away and was buried in nearby Greenwood Cemetery. But habits are hard to break. Not even death could deter Kit Smith's sad-eyed bride from her daily pilgrimage to the widow's walk.

Over the years, people in Clarksville have seen a lady, clad all in black, pacing up and down along the widow's walk at the Smith-Trahern Mansion. She stands there silently, gazing into the horizon, waiting for Kit to return.

The Smith-Trahern Mansion, long neglected, has once more been restored, and opened to the public. The volunteers there are down to earth folk, not normally prone to fanciful tales. But many times, things still happen in the Smith-Trahern Mansion that defy logic. When opening up the house in the morning, a volunteer will sometimes find the furniture or bric-a-brac rearranged—even though the house had been locked up tight. The Ladies often joke that "Lucy" has been re-decorating again!—and who is to say she has not? Clarksville, Tennessee, is less than an hour north of Nashville, and only a short distance west of Adams, Tennessee, home of the infamous Bell Witch.

For more information write: Smith-Trahern Mansion, P.O. Box 852, Clarksville, TN, 37043, (931) 648-9998.

35

CONFEDERATE HILL

Not all ghosts associated with the Civil War are found in the South, nor did all die during the war. Union prisoner of war camps certainly did more than their fair share to contribute to the mortality rate during the war, and elsewhere in the land one can occasionally encounter singular occurrences that seem to defy easy category.

Iowa, for example, is not often thought of as a state that one associates with the Civil War—much less with phantom rebels. However, if one can give credence to contemporary reports, it was home to at least one such phantom Johnny Reb.

In the era following the War Between the States, the town of Creston, Iowa, while not the oldest, was regarded as one of the liveliest of communities in the West. The good folk of that town, as a rule, were concerned with the nuts and bolts of living, and not overly concerned with things supernatural.

The end of the war had brought an influx of new settlers from the East, many of them coming to live in one of the newer districts on the east side of town, nicknamed Confederate Hill.

The toponym for the new neighborhood had begun as something in the nature of a joke. Most of the town was evenly divided as to political preferences, but in the new part of town, the Democratic Party prevailed as the people's political preference. During the war, the Republican Party had never missed an opportunity to paint the Democrats as disloyal and secessionist in outlook, as fellow travelers with the Confederate to the South, so the predominantly Democratic district was labeled "Confederate."

At one point, a local wit had even suggested that Confederate pickets should be thrown out around the district on voting day to protect the hill from intrusion by Republicans! It may also have been that, in addition to the new district's political bias, many of the new arrivals really were from the South. The South during reconstruction was not a very pleasant place to live for many, and large numbers of Southerners migrated westward after the war. So there may have been more than a few gray-clad graybeards who moved there to live—and die.

Some years after the war, it happened that a citizen from the Republican part of town was passing by the bottom of Confederate Hill one evening, walking home in the dark. Walking briskly along the road, Mr. Jones was suddenly challenged by a hollow sounding voice from out of the dark:

"Halt! Who goes there?" it cried.

Jones was startled by the unexpected challenge. His surprise turned to terror when a ghostly figure blocked his path. The apparition was clothed in a uniform of butternut—a brown drab colored uniform common to the Confederate forces late in the war. The uniform was butternut, alright, but its regimentals were rotting away, exposing what passed for flesh underneath— more bone than flesh. The figure was gaunt and skeletal-like, and reeked of decay and mold. The figure was armed with a rusted old musket, which he proceeded to aim at Jones. He could hear the click of hammer cocking as the phantom Reb prepared to fire at him.

"Don't shoot!" cried Jones.

With that, the wraith let loose a mocking laugh and approaching closer, grinned a bony smile. Then, he vanished right before Jones' eyes! In abject terror, Jones ran back towards the center of town, to a local watering hole called Summit House. A popular gathering place for the male population of town, Jones repaired there to gain reinforcements—and refreshment.

Mr. Jones related all that had befallen him that night, not leaving out a detail or fact; yet instead of sympathy, howls of laughter and scorn greeted his recounting of the late encounter. His veracity and his manhood impugned, he dared any of them to go back with him to confront the apparition again.

The crowd—fortified one suspects by liquid courage—jumped at the offer to become ghostbusters, or more likely, to extract more humor from the situation. The posse followed Jones back to Confederate Hill. By now the moon had risen, shining its pallid illumination on the scene. They hid themselves in a ravine near where Jones said he had first encountered the ghost. They did not have long to wait. In the ghostly gray light, the phantom sentinel was seen approaching. He was as Jones had described; clad in butternut, with tattered cuffs and collar, armed with a rusty old musket. The phantom rebel paced a full fifty yards, then turned about-face and marched back the same distance, as if on sentry duty.

One of the party suggested they get closer, to see who it is. Trembling as they crept forward, the men came within a hundred feet before the challenge rang out:

"Halt! Who goes there!" said the phantom.

One of the more quick-witted of the crowd called back, "Friends of the Cause."

With that, the apparition emitted a weird, demented laugh. Some in the crowd thought they heard him answer, "What Cause?" Others thought he said, "The Cause is Lost!" in an almost hysterical tone. With that, however, the phantom let loose a blood-curdling rebel yell and as the sound faded from their ears, so too did the apparition before their eyes. The would-be ghost hunters had been successful, but were now a far more sober bunch than before—ghosts have a way of doing that to folks.

The friends of Mr. Jones, in the end, decided to keep quiet about the affair, fearing no one would believe them, or worse, that the town would think them crazy.

Many years later, the story leaked out and was carried by a prominent midwestern newspaper. When all is said and done, the haunting of Confederate Hill in Union County, Iowa, remains a unique and unexplainable encounter with the ghosts and haunts of the Civil War.

36

AFTER THE STORM—
A RAINBOW

It was the early spring of 1865 when it happened. Like his neighbors, Jesse Smith, an elderly farmer, was waiting for word from the front. The war had raged through Kentucky and the rest of the South for four long years. Demossville had its defenders of the Union and supporters of secession like everywhere else in Kentucky—and men like old Jesse who were smart enough to keep their mouths shut when it came to politics. By now, supporters of both sides were weary of the strife, weary of all the killing, and most folks just longed for an end to it all.

Jesse Smith's farm was well known throughout the community, and he was respected for his honesty and integrity. One April morning, a severe storm tore through the community, wreaking havoc, destroying property, and injuring folks randomly. It was a terrifying ordeal, but like all tempests it came to an end.

When the storm passed, Smith and his wife were dumbfounded at what they saw. A brilliant rainbow had appeared in the panes of their front window. Invisible from within, from the outside one could see that all three panes on the lower part of the window bore light-hued colors. The rainbow was in full color, each band of its arc measuring some six inches wide. The colors had not been painted on or stained in any way; yet they were bright and somehow embedded in the glass itself.

The rainbow's appearance created a near panic in the community. Folks began to say it was an omen having to do with the war. Just as one suffers through the lightning and thunder and is rewarded with a beautiful rainbow in the heavens—harbinger of peace and tranquillity—so too with this more mysterious visitor.

Kentucky, and the nation as a whole, had suffered the storm of war, the thunder of the cannon's roar, and the lightning flashes of thousands of muskets firing. Now this rainbow had appeared mysteriously out of nowhere on the Smith farm, and it too was widely hailed as a harbinger of peace. Of old, the rainbow was regarded as a divine messenger. Given the strange circumstances surrounding the appearance of this rainbow on the Smith farm, it was easy enough to make that leap of faith.

The rainbow in the window was a wonderment, to be sure. Whether it was truly supernatural remains a moot point. Yet within a short time of the rainbow's appearance, news arrived which served to confirm the belief in it as a presentment of the first magnitude. Word arrived of General Lee's surrender, Lincoln's assassination, and the capitulation of Joe Johnston's army in the Carolinas. No matter which side you were on, it was news of both sadness and joy. Within a short time peace was at last restored and the war began to fade into history.

For decades, the rainbow remained as bright as the day it first appeared; a continuing reminder that no matter how terrible the tempest, peace will endure.

APPENDIX I:
CIVIL WAR GHOST TOURS

In recent years, organized ghost tours have sprouted up all over the South. Some cities that abound with ghosts, such as Charleston, Savannah, and New Orleans, have surprisingly few Civil War ghosts. Other towns that are rife with them—such as Franklin, Tennessee—have no organized tours to inform outsiders about their numerous spectral residents.

Following are a few notable ghosts tours for those wishing to explore the supernatural Civil War in person.

Farnsworth House Mourning Theater and Farnsworth House Candlelight Ghost Walks

401 Baltimore Street
Gettysburg, PA 17325
(717) 334-8838
e-mail: farnhaus@mail.cvn.net

It's the original Gettysburg ghost tour, and by all accounts one of the best. Patty O'Day is in charge of Farnsworth House, itself a most spectrally enhanced facility; Cindy Shultz, a sixth generation Gettysburger, operates the candlelight tour in season.

Ghosts of Gettysburg Candlelight Walking Tours

P.O. Box 3126
Gettysburg, PA 17325
(717) 337-0445

One of the more popular of the many ghost tours of Gettysburg, this is based on the series of booklets by Mark Nesbitt on Gettysburg's ghosts and haunts.

Ghost Tours of Harpers Ferry

Route 1, Box 468
Harpers Ferry, WV 25425
(304) 725-8019

This is one of the first Civil War ghost tours in the nation, and it's still going strong. Conducted spring, summer, and fall.

Call Petersburg Ghost Tours for a current schedule: (804) 733-2401.

Petersburg Department of Tourism

15 West Bank Street
Petersburg, VA 28303
(804) 733-2401

Center Hill Mansion

15 West Bank Street
Petersburg, VA 28303
(804) 733-2401

An annual Halloween Cemetery Walk is held on October 31. In addition, Center Hill Mansion holds a ghost watch on January 24, the day of the Phantom Regiment's traditional parade. Center Hill Mansion is owned and operated by the Petersburg Department of Tourism.

The Casemate Museum

P.O. Box 51341
Casemate 20, Bernard Road
Fort Monroe, VA 23651
(757) 727-3973

Fort Monroe is still an active army base, but the museum is open to the public.

During October and at Christmastime the Museum conducts Lantern Tours of the Fort. The emphasis is on life in the fort during the nineteenth century, but does mention some of the fort's many spectral residents.

McRaven Tour Home

1445 Harrison Street
Vicksburg, MS 39180
(601) 636-1663

One of the more spectrally enhanced places in a city brimming with ghosts of the past. Open five days a week in the fall and spring, and seven days a week from June through August. Call for hours and tour information.

Point Lookout State Park

P.O. Box 48
Scottland, MD 20687
(301) 872-5688

Located in St. Mary's County at the extreme southern end of the peninsula where the Chesapeake meets the Potomac. Though there is no organized ghost tour here, the park staff is generally more forthcoming about the ghosts and hauntings of the park and its surrounding area than the average park personnel.

Appendix II:
Haunted Hotels
of the Civil War

The following is only a partial listing of inns, bed and breakfasts, and hotels that have one or more Civil War ghosts among their guests. In some cases, the management promotes the supernatural aspects of their facility, and in others they would rather not discuss it. Either way, when staying at any of these places, the normal rules of hospitality apply for guests as well as host. And whatever you do—please don't scare the ghosts!

GEORGIA
Barnsley Gardens Inn and Resort
597 Barnsley Gardens Road
Adairsville, GA 30103
(770) 773-7480

One of Georgia's more famous haunted plantations, the original mansion is in ruins, but the famed gardens are still intact. A new inn and resort has recently been completed on the plantation grounds, keeping with the design of the original gardens. Wisely, they avoided building near the Indian mound that started the original haunting. Among the many ghosts of Barnsley Gardens is at least one of Civil War vintage.

LOUISIANA
Lloyd Hall Plantation
292 Lloyd Bridge Road
Cheneyville, LA 71325
(318) 776-5641

This antebellum bed and breakfast has six guest rooms and features Harry, a young Yankee soldier who fell in love with the wrong planter's daughter and was beaten to death. The Yankees hung William Lloyd in reprisal. Now both haunt the grounds.

Myrtles Plantation
P.O. Box 1100
St. Francisville, LA 70775
(225) 635-6277

Described by one writer as America's most haunted house, this ten-room antebellum bed and breakfast at last count boasted no less than fourteen ghosts, including one Confederate and three Union ghosts. Ask about their cook Chloe's special cake mix; it's a recipe to die for.

Olivier House
828 Toulouse
New Orleans, LA 70112
(504) 525-8456

Built in 1836, this forty-two room hotel is located in the heart of the French Quarter. It is said to be haunted by a Confederate soldier and his sweetheart, who have been reported making out in various parts of the hotel.

175

MARYLAND
The Piper House
P.O. Box 100
Sharpsburg, MD 21782
(301) 797-1862

This small bed and breakfast is located right on the field of battle itself. Civil War ghosts have been reported here by both Troy Taylor's *Ghosts of the Prairie* magazine and Wilmer Mumma's book on Antietam ghosts, but the owners of the house dismiss it all as folklore. They say they have never had spectral encounters and put no stock in any stories in that regard. Still, this cozy bed and breakfast, with three guest rooms, is ideal for anyone wishing to get right into the spirit of the Battle of Antietam.

MISSISSIPPI
Anchuca
1010 First East Street
Vicksburg, MS 39180
(601) 661-0111

In Choctaw, Anchuca means "happy home," and a stay here will certainly put a smile on one's face, ghosts or no ghosts. Jefferson Davis delivered a speech to the citizens of the city from Anchuca's balcony, and his brother Joseph lived here after the Yankees burned his plantation. The present owner, Loveta Byrne, was unaware of the house's spectral heritage, although she says she did own a house in Natchez that was haunted. This antebellum home has a master bedroom and five other guest rooms, as well as a swimming pool, hot tubs, and all the mint juleps you can sip. The house has several

ghosts, some of which are believed to be of Civil War vintage.

Cedar Grove Mansion Inn
2200 Oak Street
Vicksburg, MS 39180
(601) 636-1000

This 1840 bed and breakfast features five guest rooms in the main house, plus outbuildings, and when contacted the staff verified that the house is indeed haunted. This house was used as Federal headquarters when Grant occupied the city in July, 1863, and the room he slept in is one of the guest rooms, with all the original furnishings.

Duff-Green Mansion
1114 First East Street
Vicksburg, MS 39180
(601) 636-6968

Built in 1856, this mansion served as a hospital for wounded Confederates during the siege. The suffering spirits of these men resound in its four walls.

Harbour Oaks Inn
126 West Scenic Drive
Pass Christian, MS 39571
(228) 452-9399

Located on the gulf coast, during the war it was the Crescent Hotel, which in turn was converted into a hospital. A number of phantoms have been sighted here, The phantom of "the fellas" was particularly active until the house was "cleansed," and now only the more docile spirits remain.

PENNSYLVANIA
Cashtown Inn
P.O. Box 103
Cashtown, PA 17310
(717) 334-9722

Located near Gettysburg, the Cashtown Inn has been home to at least one Confederate ghost for the last 135 years. The seven-room bed and breakfast was featured in the movie *Gettysburg* and the video *Ghosts of Gettysburg*.

Farnsworth House
401 Baltimore Street
Gettysburg, PA 17325
(717) 334-8838

Located in the heart of Gettysburg, this bed and breakfast also has a tavern on premises, as well as gift shops and a "mourning theatre" in the basement. A number of ghosts inhabit Farnsworth, including several Confederates; some of the staff have also experienced the phenomenon of retrocognition. Time warp, anyone? A must-see for any ghosthunter visiting Gettysburg.

TENNESSEE
Loretta Lynn's Dude Ranch and Campgrounds
44 Hurricane Mills Road
Hurricane Mills, TN 37078
(931) 296-7700

Located an hour west of Nashville. When Loretta Lynn bought this large antebellum mansion overlooking the hamlet of Hurricane Mills in 1967, she had no inkling the place was haunted. Under the porch, she and her husband, Mooney, found a cramped stone cellar that turned out to be a "slave pit." Occasionally they still hear moans, rattling chains, and the sound of feet shuffling in leg irons. Several Civil War soldiers are buried on the grounds, and their spirits are believed to haunt the house as well.

Read House
827 Broad Street
Chattanooga, TN 37402
(423) 266-4121

The 238-room hotel was not built until 1926, but it was constructed on the foundations of an earlier structure, which served as a hotel during the Civil War. The ghosts of that earlier era are believed to haunt Read House. During the war, allegedly a Union soldier murdered a prostitute there; he was court-martialed and executed, and now his restless shade returns to the site of his crime. If you are particularly brave, or foolish, ask for room 311.

VIRGINIA
Edgewood Plantation
4800 John Tyler Highway
Charles City, VA 23030
(804) 829-2962

While having eight guest rooms, this 1849 bed and breakfast has some seven thousand square feet to wander about in, plus a grist mill and assorted outbuildings. Also wandering about is Lizzie, still waiting for her lover to return.

Martha Washington Inn
150 West Main Street
Abingdon, VA 24210
(540) 628-3161

During the Civil War, this was Martha Washington College, a finishing school for fine young ladies of quality. During the war, it was converted into a hospital and both Union and Confederate soldiers were treated there. One young Yankee developed a special relationship with one of the young Rebel nurses, and when he died, she pined away for him—and to this day she still pines away for him. Also present is a ghost-horse, whose master was killed in battle.

Wayside Inn

7783 Main Street
Middletown, VA 22645
(540) 869-1797

Originally known as Wilkinson's Tavern, the oldest part of this twenty-four-room rustic inn dates to 1742. By the time of the Civil War it was called Larrick's Hotel, and as such it saw the passing of the armies during Stonewall Jackson's legendary Valley Campaign and also the aftermath of the Battle of Cedar Creek in 1864. Like many other buildings in the area, it was used as a temporary field hospital. People have seen Civil War soldiers milling about in the lobby and others have heard footsteps of invisible soldiers pacing the hallways.

Willow Grove

14079 Plantation Way
Orange, VA 22960
(540) 672-5982

This ten-room bed and breakfast, situated on thirty-seven acres in the scenic rolling hills of Virginia, is only minutes from Thomas Jefferson's Monticello (also haunted, but we won't go into that here). It's also light years away from the stress and pressures of modern life. Built in 1778, the house is on the National Register and the grounds are often used by Civil War reenactors. The inn has seven guest rooms, a restaurant, and a tavern featuring upscale Southern cuisine. The innkeeper since 1987 has been Angela Malloy, and she and her husband believe that much of the paranormal activity folks have reported here is connected with the house's occupation by both armies during the Civil War.

In particular, a phantom Confederate soldier has been observed paying court to a spectral southern belle, proving that even death is no barrier to true love. The ghost of a slave woman, allegedly murdered by her master before the war, has also been seen on the grounds. Some guests have even had conversations with her.